WEST COAST WALKS

KNOYDART, SKYE
and
WESTER ROSS

WEST COAST WALKS

KNOYDART, SKYE
and
WESTER ROSS

Pamela Clark

KITTIWAKE

Published by
Kittiwake Press
3 Glantwymyn Village Workshops, Machynlleth,
Montgomeryshire SY20 8LY

First edition 2000
© Text: Pamela Clark 2000
© Maps: Kittiwake 2000

Every care has been taken to make the information,
walk descriptions and maps as accurate as possible
but neither the author or the publisher can accept any
responsibility for errors, however caused.
The countryside is always changing and land ownership
may alter access, so there will inevitably be alterations
to some aspects of these walks in future. If you would
like to help keep this book up to date, please send
your comments to the above address.

Please remember that much land is private. Inclusion
in this book does not imply any right of public access.

Roads and tracks indicated are not necessarily
rights of way. If in doubt, seek permission first.

Produced on an Apple Macintosh using Adobe Photoshop,
Macromedia Freehand and QuarkXPress.

The typeface is Melior.

Film output by
WPG, Welshpool, Montgomeryshire

Printed by
MFP Design & Print, Manchester

A catalogue record for this book may be found in the British Library

ISBN 1 902302 03 6

Cover photographs: Main picture: Evening light at Ardban, Applecross;
inset: Eilean Donan Castle

INTRODUCTION

The west coast of Scotland between Mallaig and Ullapool is one of the most dramatic and beautiful parts of Europe. A land indented by long sea lochs with a myriad of islands and fringed with quiet white-sand beaches or stunning rocky shores and precipitous cliffs, leading inland to empty moorland, deeply carved glacial valleys and high rugged mountains sweeping down to the sea. During the Highland Clearances of the 18th and 19th centuries, people were callously evicted to make way for sheep. This along with the rugged nature of the terrain itself, is largely responsible for the area being generally sparsely populated with a series of secluded coastal villages and scattered crofts. Those who remain, eke out a living mainly from tourism, fishing, crofting, crafts and forestry. Its relative remoteness has resulted in a tremendous range of wildlife thriving, unequalled elsewhere in Britain. With a great range of flora and fauna habitats, found often in close proximity, botanists too will find a paradise. Anglers will be spoilt for choice in their search for excellent freshwater and sea fishing whilst experienced yachtsmen will find a surfeit of challenging waters.

With a lack of roads across much of the region, the only way to really explore is on foot or by boat. The purpose of this book is to be both a tourist and walking guide, catering for all; from the visitor who likes the occasional easy stroll to the hardened hillwalker who also likes to be more of a general tourist on a rest day from the mountains. A number of ascents of Munros and Corbetts have been included. For those unfamiliar with these terms, a Munro is one of the 284 mountains in Scotland over 3000 feet, first surveyed and listed by Sir Hugh Munro in 1891. A Corbett is one of the 221 hills between 2500 – 3000 feet with a reascent of at least 500 feet on all sides between adjoining hills. Ticking off all the Corbetts has not gained the popularity that climbing all the Munros has (Munro bagging) and subsequently makes for much quieter hills but no less outstanding viewpoints. Along with many gentle walks, some lesser hill ascents are also described, which provide equally fine views.

The first book in this series follows the coast from Oban to Mallaig. This book continues north from Mallaig to Ullapool. Essential tourist information is given on places of interest and on what and where non walking activities can be enjoyed and availability of public transport. Within the text and listed in the appendix, are the locations of Tourist Information Centres in the area. These are invaluable, being the most up to date sources of local information on available accommodation and restaurants, times of public transport, availability of day excursions, boat charters and opening times of tourist facilities. The appendix also has useful phone numbers for a large range of outdoor enthusiasts. The tourist section has no long glowing scenic descriptions. The whole vast area is very beautiful; every drive a breathtaking experience. It is better to go and explore it for yourself. Scenic highlights that could easily be missed are mentioned, however.

Over sixty scenic walking routes are described in the book, ranging from half hour strolls to full day strenuous walks in the mountains and along the coast. Virtually every hard walk finishes with a suggested easier option, within the same locality, for the less energetic. No-one on their holiday should be at a loss for where to go for a rewarding walk. The majority provide views of the sea at some point, although a few keep to sheltered forest trails and glens where the main objective is usually to reach a beautiful waterfall: ideal destinations when the weather is too inclement for the coasts and hills. The Isle of Skye has been included, though only in the walks section, having been covered in the sister publication, *The Western Islands Handbook*. However, many of the tourist sites are included within the text of the walks. Skye is easily visited on a day trip by those staying near Glenelg or Kyle of Lochalsh, although to see the best of the island it is worth staying there for at least a few days.

All of the easier walking routes follow tracks and paths, though many of the hillwalks and some coastal hikes have long pathless sections. Unlike in England and Wales, very few Scottish mountains have cairned or easy to follow paths all the way up, adding to the challenge and sense of adventure. Cairns are only usually found on the highest points. Hillwalkers therefore must be competent in the use of map and compass. Also, unlike most of their southern and eastern counterparts, most hillwalks in western Scotland start at or close to sea level, so a certain level of fitness is required. Another difference is the lack of bridges across many rivers, so it is advisable to be familiar with river crossing techniques. Snow can linger on the summits well into April and occasionally into May, so competence with ice axe and crampons will be required at such times. All walkers should carry good waterproof clothing and wear stout footwear. In addition, hillwalkers should carry a spare top, map, compass, torch, whistle, basic first-aid kit and adequate food and drink. It is advisable to leave word of your route with someone and expected time back, particularly if hillwalking alone.

It is important to bear in mind that the weather can change very rapidly and dramatically. It is not unusual to experience all four seasons within a few hours! The west coast climate is generally mild and wet and unpredictable. From the author's experience (and to some extent, statistics back this up), usually the best time to visit is from late April to the end of June, when in most years there is a dry-ish period lasting 6 – 8 weeks. There is often a long settled spell in October as well. At other times you will generally experience far more wet days than dry, though just occasionally, there is drought for much of the summer. Late April and May are particularly attractive, not only with the drier weather and very long daylight hours, but because of the lack of midges. These wee pests do not usually start biting until early June. In late spring too, the woods are carpeted with bluebells and primroses and the vibrant greens of the valleys contrast with the northern corries and mountain summits still fringed white with snow. Autumn is particularly beautiful, with the coming of the first summit snows, the rowan trees in full fruit and the trees and bracken turning colour. The midges also are dying away.

Roads are often narrow and can be single track, requiring careful and considerate driving. By avoiding the height of summer, driving is much more pleasurable. Allow plenty of time for your journey and be aware that petrol stations are often far apart and generally closed in the evening and on Sundays. If circumstances dictate that you have to visit during busier July and August, by using this book you can get well off the beaten track and find natural tranquillity. Just remember the waterproofs and insect repellent!

As you explore the area, take care to respect the land and its people, flora and fauna. This remains one of the most unspoilt areas of Europe. Long may it remain so.

Pam Clark

TOURIST INFORMATION

KNOYDART TO SHIEL BRIDGE

North of Mallaig, much of the coastal fringe is extremely indented and totally roadless, necessitating long detours to reach the head of the lochs. This is particularly true of Lochs Nevis and Hourn, the lochs of heaven and hell. Sandwiched between them is the Knoydart Peninsula, one of Scotland's remotest and wildest regions, only reachable by boat or on foot. Sheep farming, deer stalking and forestry are for the moment, the mainstays for the small population based at **Inverie** on Loch Nevis. Recent and frequent changes of absentee landowners have created an atmosphere of uncertainty over the viability and future of the Knoydart Estate. Mallaig is reached by following the long Road to the Isles from Fort William (also served by regular rail & bus services). *Four days a week*, mailboat sailings from Mallaig take passengers to Tarbert and Inverie (*Mon, Wed, Fri, Sat*). (Note that the boat no longer drops at Camusrory). Inverie boasts a post office/shop, a pub and a variety of accommodation. Generally good paths and tracks radiate out into the five main glens of the peninsula and above its western shore, making for easy though remote walking. By contrast, all of Knoydart's mountains are extremely rough and virtually pathless offering challenging and breathtaking hikes recommended only to experienced walkers.

To reach one of the two road heads on the fringes of Knoydart or to rejoin the west coast, one must head north on the A82 through Fort William and Spean Bridge. Just beyond the Commando Memorial above Spean Bridge, the B8004 bears left to Gairlochy and the loch gates on the Caledonian Canal at the outflow of Loch Lochy. The B8005 continues to Clunes and **Loch Arkaig.** At Achnacarry House there is the **Clan Cameron Museum** (*daily Easter – mid Oct*) which recounts the sad tale of Cameron of Locheil and his clan who were staunch supporters of Bonnie Prince Charlie in the Jacobite Campaign of 1745 – 46 which attempted to claim the British Crown. There are also exhibits about the Commandos who trained in the area during World War II.

The road passes the wooded 'Dark Mile' and the fine double waterfall of Chia-Aig. During August 1746 after the Battle of Culloden, Bonnie Prince Charlie hid for a fortnight in this area. His hiding places included a tree, long gone and a cave some 800 feet up the hillside. He made his escape along Loch Arkaig's southern shore. The tortuously winding road follows the well wooded north shore of this peaceful and unspoilt loch. The French brought over a large quantity of gold to support the Jacobites.

Arriving just too late to assist the cause, it was buried at Murlaggan, to prevent it falling into Government hands. Mystery has since shrouded the fate of the treasure. The road ends near Strathan beyond the head of the loch. Good tracks lead through two long, lonely passes towards the sea. The heavily afforested Glean Pean, once used by Bonnie Prince Charlie, gains Loch Morar. The higher pass of Mam na Cloich Airde at the head of **Glen Dessary,** drops 1000 feet to Loch Nevis flanked by shapely Sgurr na Ciche **(walk 1)**.

The A82 continues past hillsides of rampant rhododendrons along the lochs of the Great Glen to **Invergarry.** Here lies the remains of Glen Garry Castle, burnt by 'Butcher Cumberland' in 1746, having been used to shelter Bonnie Prince Charlie. Off-road cyclists are well catered for with waymarked (though often steep) forest tracks from Invergarry to Oich Bridge, Laggan and Gairlochy. These also offer sheltered walking when the weather further west is off-putting. Turning onto the Kyle of Lochalsh road, just west of Invergarry there is another forestry walk with a track from a car park leading past a good spate river to a loch.

Five miles west of Invergarry, a narrow, no through road turns off to Tomdoun and Kinloch Hourn. It becomes increasingly scenic. Loch Quoich is particularly attractive in late spring when the gorse and rhododendrons front the loch backed by a clutch of rugged and remote Munros (one of the scenes used on the Royal Bank of Scotland credit card). The road drops dramatically to **Kinloch Hourn** at the head of Loch Hourn, a magnificent fjord and the easiest pedestrian access point for Knoydart (see **walk 2**). Above the loch stands the superb viewpoint of Sgurr a' Mhaoraich **(walk 3)**.

The A87 progresses over high, increasingly afforested moorland towards the west coast, passing through a Munro baggers playground around Loch Cluanie and **Glen Shiel (walks 4 & 5)**. At the western head of the loch lies the remote and welcoming Cluanie Inn and Cluanie Crafts and Woollens. In lower Glen Shiel stands the site of the battle of 1719, below Sgurr nan Spainteach, 'Spaniards' Peak', named after the 300 Spanish soldiers who fought for the Jacobites against the Hanovarians. A long and disorderly skirmish ended with the Spaniards fleeing for their lives over the mountain.

GLENELG PENINSULA

At Shiel Bridge at the head of Loch Duich, a narrow road turns off for Glenelg and Corran. The reward for the climb to the head of the Mam Ratagain Pass, is a classic and stunning view of the Five Sisters of Kintail, best seen near sunset. The original road was used by drovers taking cattle and sheep from Skye down to lowland markets. It was upgraded to a military road after the first Jacobite Rising. Fort Bernera was manned from 1722 – 1790. Its ruins can still be seen near **Glenelg.** Approaching the tiny village, Glenelg Candles is past on the left, an arts and craft centre, *open March-December.* Two miles north of Glenelg, a small vehicular ferry provides frequent crossings to Kylerhea in Skye (*April – Oct, not Sunday till mid May*), for the discerning traveller for whom the new Skye bridge is an anathema (tel. 01599 511302). Seals can often be seen around the ferry and otters frequent the coast (see **walks 8 & 12**). Cattle used to be swum across this narrow channel from Skye, en route to market. The Fingalian giants of Celtic legend had a more novel approach. On their return from hunting trips in Skye, they used their huge spears as poles to leap the narrows or 'kyle.' On one such trip, Reidh's spear broke as he attempted the leap and he fell and drowned, hence 'Kylerhea' today.

A mile south of Glenelg, a road bears left into Gleann Beag and in 1.5 miles reaches the Iron Age Brochs of **Dun Telve and Dun Trodden,** built around 2000 years ago to protect the locals from raiders. They are the finest broch remains on the British mainland (**walk 9**).

Five miles southward lies Upper Sandaig. From here a rough track leads in a mile to the shore at Sandaig, once the home of writer Gavin Maxwell of 'Ring of Bright Water' fame. He instructed that the house be destroyed upon his death and his ashes be placed under a boulder. Otters still thrive along these shores. Beyond the forests, a dramatic chocolate box prospect opens out to Loch Hourn, dominated by Ladhar Bheinn and Beinn Sgritheall (**walk 10**). From the tiny village of **Arnisdale,** a year round occasional ferry provides the easiest access to Barrisdale in Knoydart. Trips are also offered on Loch Hourn (tel. 01599 522352). A mile on the road ends at **Corran,** (teashop and B & B), the starting point for an easy and beautiful coastal outing (**walk 11**). The hamlet is reachable by a once daily postbus from Kyle of Lochalsh.

LOCH DUICH TO KYLE OF LOCHALSH

The main road from Shiel Bridge heads along Loch Duich. A road forks right to Morvich and Dorusduain (see **walks 6 & 7**). The **Scottish National Trust Countryside Centre** at Morvich (*May – Sept daily*) houses an audiovisual exhibition describing the work of the Kintail Estate and giving advice on local walks. **Loch Long** flows into **Loch Duich at the small village of Dornie**, a good base for fishing the surrounding lochs. The no through road along Loch Long provides pedestrian access to picturesque **Glen Elchaig** and the spectacular **Falls of Glomach** (**walk 7**).

Close to Dornie at the beautiful confluence of Lochs Alsh, Long and

Duich lies **Eilean Donan,** one of the most photographed castles in Britain, (*open daily Easter – Oct*). A triple arched causeway leads to the medieval castle, originally built in 1230 for King Alexander II of Scotland on the site of an ancient vitrified fort. It was first used as a stronghold by the Mackenzies, the Earl of Seaforth, against the raiding Vikings from Skye. At the time of the Battle of Glen Shiel in 1719, Spanish troops were garrisoned here in support of the Jacobites. As a consequence, it was bombarded by English men-of-war and badly damaged. Restored by the Macleans in the 1930's, it now has a two-room museum with many Jacobite exhibits.

Six miles along the coast, the Scottish National Trust has been bequeathed the **Balmacara Estate.** An enchanting though still developing woodland garden has been laid out above the shore of Loch Alsh, with well constructed woodland paths allowing easy access and delightful, sheltered walking (*open daily 9am – sunset*). *Every Tuesday during July and August*, ranger guided evening walks are organised. Tel. 01599 566325 for booking and further details.

The A87 terminates in 3 miles at Kyle of Lochalsh, a fishing port and important tourist and route centre with the new controversial bridge to Skye, rail connections to Inverness and bus services to Glasgow, Fort William, Inverness and Skye. Kyle largely developed with the coming of the railway from Dingwall in 1897. The line's history is as colourful as the scenery through which it passes. The Victorian visionary behind it was Alexander Matheson, who made a fortune through the opium trade between India and China. He returned to Scotland and persuaded other Highland lairds to back his scheme. For 27 years the line terminated at Stromeferry. It required Government grants after Matheson's death to finally push the line through to Kyle. Some 900 navvies were involved in the construction and blasting of 31 huge cuttings up to 65 feet deep. It became the most expensive stretch of line in the country. Important for tourism, the line was also used during the World Wars for transportation of stores, men and munitions when Kyle was one of a number of important naval bases in northern Scotland.

Kyle is not pretty in itself but lies in a lovely setting and provides a good range of tourist facilities. These include a tourist information office (*April – Oct*), a 9 hole golf course, year round 'Seafood Cruises', wildlife trips, boat hire and charter from the harbour (tel. 01599 577230) and a swimming pool at Douglas Park. The tidal race off Loch Alsh is good for shore fishing, especially sea trout and mackerel though the race needs to be treated with caution by inexperienced sea anglers and yachtsmen. Many hill lochs in the area can be fished for brown trout free of charge. Contact the Tourist Information Centre for details.

PLOCKTON, LOCH CARRON

The main road north turns off the A87 near Auchtertyre east of Balmacara. The most scenic route however turns off at Balmacara Square and heads over the hills to Durinish and Plockton, affording fine views to Applecross. Half a mile beyond Duirinish as the road begins to descend to Plockton, walkers with 30 minutes to spare should turn right and park at the head of the rise ahead. About 100 yards west of the high point of the road, an obvious path heads north through the heather and bracken to gain the east ridge and summit of Creag nan Caradh (GR 802328). This 400 yard walk affords superb vistas over Plockton harbour to Applecross and Skye (note that the path is occasionally rough underfoot & initially can be boggy).

Beautiful **Plockton** village, complete with neat white houses, wooded crags, palm trees and sheltered harbour, is popular with artists, yachtsmen and fans of TV's Hamish MacBeth. Boat and canoe hire is available. Highly scenic, short wildlife / seal cruises are offered from the harbour: contact **Castle Moil Cruises** (*April – Oct*) tel. 01599 544235 and **Leisure Marine** (*April – Sept*) tel. 01599 544306.

The road from Plockton to the main road near Achmore and Stromeferry, passes **Craig Highland Farm,** an animal sanctuary and rare breeds farm, open to the public (*March – Oct*). Near Achmore, one can sample fine cheeses at the **West Highland Dairy** (*open all year*).

Strome Woods offer easy sheltered walking with fine views over Loch Carron from waymarked Forestry Commission trails. Turn off the A890 for Stromeferry. A car park and picnic area lies 400 yards downhill on the left.

The main road climbs high above Loch Carron before descending to hug the shoreline cheek by jowl with the railway. The remarkable and expensive feat of Victorian engineering can really be appreciated here, where they had to blast through solid rock for great distances. Set back from the loch, **Attadale Gardens and Woodland** walks are open to the public *April – Oct Mon – Sat*. Begun in the 1890's, the mature gardens and woodland are home to over 2000 species of trees and shrubs, set in delightful surroundings. Two miles on at the hamlet of **Strathcarron,** there is a stained glass studio. The more active can hire boats, canoes and fishing gear (tel. Ross Rentals 01520 722205).

Beyond the River Carron, the A890 turns right and follows the railway up the 20 mile length of Glen Carron to Achnasheen and the fast road to Inverness. The glen boasts many fine rivers and mountains. **Walk 28** samples the finest of the rivers and waterfalls whilst **walk 29** ventures into the remote mountains of the Attadale Forest.

The coastal road turns left at the T junction at the foot of Glen Carron and soon passes a picturesque 9 hole golf course and the long straggling line of houses and B & B's of **Lochcarron** village. Here, the **Smithy Heritage Centre** (*mid-April – mid-Oct. Mon – Sat*) is set in an old smithy with video and historical panels. Two miles down the road to Strome, **Lochcarron Weavers** has flourished since 1938 and now stocks the world's largest range of tartans in their mill shop. Weaving demonstrations are given throughout the year (*Mon – Fri*). **Strome Castle** lies on a small headland a further mile down the road. Unfortunately little survives. It was held by the MacDonnells of Glengarry who fought bloody feuds with the Mackenzies of Kintail. The Mackenzies ultimately captured and destroyed the castle in 1603. On the western fringe of Lochcarron, opposite the turning for Strome, lies a bridge over the River Carnan and the start of a nature reserve (**walk 30**).

APPLECROSS

The A896 from Lochcarron climbs westward over a high pass before descending to the houses of Kishorn. The loch still bears traces of the huge oil rig construction yard that thrived in the 1970s & 1980s. Turning north, the road is dominated to the west by the magnificent corries of **Beinn Bhan** (**walk 31**). To the east, a mile beyond Tornapress, lies **Raasal Ashwood,** the most northerly in Britain. This offers easy walking amidst a rich variety of flora and fauna. The route continuing north over moorland to **Shieldaig** and **Upper Loch Torridon**, misses the drama of the **Applecross Peninsula.**

The shortest and most spectacular route to **Applecross** village, bears west at **Tornapress** and climbs past rugged cliff-girt buttresses, over the notorious **Bealach nan Bo** (the pass of the cattle): at 2054 feet, the second highest road in the country. The former cattle drovers route is alpine in character, being narrow and twisting with gradients up to 1:4 and tight hairpin bends near its summit. Although greatly improved recently, it is still not for the faint hearted and can lead to an overheated engine on a scorching day. The reward is a stunning prospect across Loch Carron and over the Minch to Skye and Raasay. From the car park at the head of the pass, an easy track on the right leads in 0.75 mile to the communications mast on Sgurr a' Ghaorachain, an excellent viewpoint on the brink of the eastern cliffs.

The descent to **Applecross** is less stressful on the driver though equally narrow. Applecross Bay is a charming place in sunshine with the wooded grounds of Applecross House backing the huge banks of gorse and sandy beach looking out to the mountains of Skye (see **walk 32**). The House gardens are open to the public during the summer. The small peaceful village was an important centre of early Christianity until the Vikings destroyed the monastery founded here in 673 by the Irish monk, Maelrubha. A church now stands on the site. A stone slab carved with a cross at the churchyard entrance and several fragments of crosses inside the church, probably date from the original monastery. Like so much of the area, the Highland Clearances were largely responsible for decimating a population of around 3000 in the 19th century, to the present 200. A scenic road continues south for 4 miles along the coast, ending at the pretty harbour at **Toscaig** (**walk 33**).

Turning northward, the newer road winds its way through scattered crofting settlements above the coast on the long but breathtaking passage to Shieldaig. Views to Skye, Raasay, Rona and Lewis, give way to the rugged vistas over Loch Torridon, one of the most striking sea lochs in the country.

TORRIDON

Shieldaig is a small, picture postcard fishing village with encircling rough hills backing Lochs Shieldaig and Torridon and the heronry on Shieldaig Island. There are facilities for sea fishing with catches including skate, sea trout, whiting and haddock. It was here in 1893 that the minister broke with the established church and joined with the minister from Raasay to form the Free Presbyterian Church which is still very alive today. A short coastal walk affording excellent views of the loch, begins at the war memorial (**walk 34**).

Two miles eastward along the loch, the **Falls of Balgy** are easily reached from the road bridge, a worthwhile detour when the river is in spate (see end **walk 35**). Beyond a high viewpoint with a grandiose view across the loch of Beinn Alligin and Liathach, the road descends to the massed rhododendrons surrounding the hamlet of **Annat,** the start point for several fine hikes (**walks 35 & 36**).

At the road junction a mile beyond, a **Scottish National Trust Visitor Centre** provides information on the mountains, flora and fauna of the Torridon area; a mecca for walkers and climbers. Closeby is the small **Deer Museum**. Every *Wednesday and Friday during July and August*, ranger guided walks are ideal for inexperienced hillwalkers reluctant to tackle the gripping **Torridon** peaks on their own (tel. 01445 791221 for booking & further details). They should certainly be treated with great respect and left to experts under winter conditions. These massive leviathans rise up abruptly from the loch and rough moorland. Miles of tiered sandstone buttresses of almost overwhelming steepness, riven by deep gullies are topped with sharply pinnacled ridges, seemingly as impregnable as a medieval fortress.

The road forks left to **Torridon** (shop, youth hostel, campsite, B & B's), Inveralligin and Diabaig. Am Ploc, the narrow promontory near the jetty, is site of a former open-air church complete with pulpit rock. During the Norse occupation some 800 years ago, it was probably home to a Norse parliament (or tingvollr) and judiciary. Most of the surrounding villages and names are corrupted from Norse. Immediately west of Torridon village is Fasag, another reminder of the Highland Clearances. In the early 19th century, evicted families were moved to poor strips of land by the coast, Fasag was one such site. Some 2.5 miles up the road, a large National Trust car park marks the start of the ascent of **Beinn Alligin** and a magnificent valley walk along the **Coire Mhic Nobuil (walks 37 & 38)**. The narrow carriageway continues high above the loch over bare and rocky moorland. The road ends at picturesque and sleepy **Diabaig** (also reachable by post-bus from Achnasheen), a hamlet of tidy cottages with a small pier and pebble beach fringing a bay surrounded by slabby sandstone hills and sporting the ubiquitous fish farms. Several excellent coastal walks begin here **(walks 39 & 40)**.

From Torridon, the A896 heads eastward through awesome Glen Torridon (see **walks 41 & 42**). Once past the mighty ramparts of Liathach, the glen begins to open out. A track along to **Lochs Clair & Coulin** offers a gentle and beautiful walk affording the finest prospective of **Beinn Eighe** and **Liathach (walk 43)**.

KINLOCHEWE & LOCH MAREE

Three miles beyond Loch Clair, lies the small village of **Kinlochewe,** offering accommodation, hotel restaurant, cafe and shops. The roadside and riverbanks studded with gorse and rhododendrons are resplendent in late spring and early summer, flanked by the vast slopes of Beinn Eighe and Slioch. With Torridon and Loch Maree closeby and easy access into the remote Fisherfield and Letterewe Forests, this makes an ideal centre for hillwalkers **(walk 44)**. It is served by bus from Gairloch and Achnasheen with rail connections to Inverness. The road eastward climbing Glen Docherty is slow going to Achnasheen but thereafter is a fast route to Inverness and the south.

Turning north-westward, the road to Gairloch follows the southern shore of **Loch Maree.** Some 12 miles long, wood fringed, island studded and watched over by the castellated ramparts of Slioch, it is arguably the prettiest freshwater loch in Scotland. The afforestation was once much greater. Numerous ironworks in the 17th century devoured vast acreages of oak woods for charcoal. Works remains can still be found, particularly along the north shore of the loch. The loch was once called Loch Ewe until the 7th century when St Maelrubha made the small isle of Eilean Maurighe a place of pilgrimage. The island's name and that of the loch became Maelrubha, later corrupted to Maree. A mile beyond Kinlochewe is **Aultroy Visitor Centre** (*10am – 5pm, May – Oct*) which explains the conservation work in **Beinn Eighe National Nature Reserve,** the first ever created in Britain, principally to preserve the native Scots pine and indigenous flora and fauna. (**walk 45**). There is a smaller nature reserve around Grudie Bridge at the entrance to Glen Grudie (**walks 46 & 47**).

Twelve miles from Kinlochewe, lie the **Victoria Falls,** named in honour of the sovereign who visited the spot whilst staying at the Loch Maree Hotel. There is a large car park and picnic area and several waymarked forest trails. The falls themselves are reached in under 200 yards along a good path. The four tiers are easily seen from a viewing platform. Above the upper bridge the wide river slides down a huge sandstone pavement. A few hundred yards along the road, a signed rough forestry road on the right leads down to a parking area beside the loch with picnic tables, toilets and the start of the 'Tollie Path' (**walk 48**).

GAIRLOCH, LOCH EWE, GRUINARD & LITTLE LOCH BROOM

Beyond the forests, the road descends a narrow gorge to the attractively situated small bustling tourist resort and fishing port of **Gairloch** looking to Skye and the Torridon mountains. The cod and herring stocks once so vital to the economy, never recovered from the overfishing and today fishermen depend on crabs, lobsters and prawns. Served by buses from Inverness, Ullapool and Achnasheen (rail connection), the village is home to a wide range of tourist facilities (Tourist Information Centre *all year*). The area has fine sandy beaches with safe bathing especially along the northern shore of Loch Gairloch, windsurfing, canoeing and a 9 hole golf course. Yachtsmen and sea anglers are well catered for. *Daily* angling trips leave from the pier. Short wildlife cruises provide opportunities of spotting porpoises, seals and whales. Highland Trails offer guided tours using four-wheel drive quad bikes (*Easter – Sept*). Contact 'The Anchorage' post office/craft shop at the harbour or tel. 01445 712378. In adverse weather, try the Leisure Centre (*open all year*), the 'Sail Gairloch' audio visual display and the award winning **Gairloch Heritage Museum** (*Mon – Sat. April – mid Oct*). This illustrates all aspects of life in a typical West Highland Parish from the earliest times to the present. On a small promontory just west of the golf course is An Dun, site of an Iron Age stone fort.

In fine weather, a rewarding local excursion can be made to **Redpoint** by taking the minor road (or postbus) 3.5 miles south of Gairloch. It passes the delightful sheltered anchorage at Badachro (boat hire available).

From the car park at Redpoint, it is just 200 yards to the safe beaches. Bays of bright red sand are backed by dunes and moorland with enchanting views to the Western Isles and mountains of Torridon and the Flowerdale Forest. From here a fine coastal path leads to **Diabaig (walk 40)**. Another beautiful drive heads west along Loch Gairloch before turning north to Melvaig (postbus from Gairloch). No vehicle access is allowed on the final 3 miles to **Rua Reidhe** (*roo a ree*) **Point** (except for visitors to the lighthouse hostel and a tea-room which is *open 3 afternoons a week*) but the road makes a rewarding walk in itself with an extension possible to **Camas Mor (walk 49)**. See also **walks 50 & 51,** both within a short drive of Gairloch.

Turning north east out of Gairloch, the main road climbs over moorland to a fine viewpoint overlooking Loch Maree at the finish of the 'Tollie Path' **(walk 48)** before descending to the small pretty village of **Poolewe** which offers a variety of tourist accommodation. From here, paths radiate to innumerable lonely lochs **(walk 52)** and into the truly remote interior of the Letterewe Forest, one of Europe's last great wilderness areas, ideal for hardy walkers wishing to escape the rat race. Loch Ewe has a number of safe sandy bays but in poor weather you may prefer to swim in the village pool. The short River Ewe used to be good for salmon and trout fishing as did Loch Maree but lice contamination from the fish farms is thought to have badly affected stocks. The remains of an iron smithy built in 1610, can be found on the banks of the river. One of the earliest blast furnaces in Scotland.

Closeby is the world famous **Inverewe Gardens** (*open daily*) owned by the Scottish National Trust. In 1862, Osgood Mackenzie bought a sandstone and peaty headland on the shores of Loch Ewe, totally devoid of trees. He planted a thick sheltering belt of pines and native trees then left them to grow for 20 years. Having drained and enriched the soil, he gradually built up a superb collection of exotic plants from around the world. Today it is one of the finest subtropical woodland gardens in Europe with over 2500 species of flowers, trees and shrubs. Best time for seeing the wonderful rhododendrons and azaleas is *mid May – mid June*, for the herbaceous garden, *July and August. From late April – early September*, ranger guided **wildlife walks** are offered in the area, beginning at the garden. Tel. 01445 781200 or Tourist Information Centres for full details).

The no through road on the west side of **Loch Ewe** leads to Cove where a deep cave was used as a place of worship until late in the 19th centuary (postbus from Poolewe). An old gun site can be found at the high point of the road, a reminder of World War II when the loch was an important naval base. The road affords excellent views across the loch to the Sutherland mountains. With patience, otters and grey and common seals can all be seen along this coast.

The main road continues north above Loch Ewe. A minor road bears left to the small harbour of Aultbea. Aultbea wood turning workshop and craft shop is open all year (*Mon – Sat*). In a further 2.5 miles is **Laide** looking out to Gruinard Bay. Just east of the tiny village, a cliff path leads to two caves. The largest was used as a Presbyterian Church meeting place until the mid 19th century. A smaller cave was refuge to families evicted from their homes during the Clearances. North of Laide, a minor road leads to the pretty bay at Mellon Udrigle, starting point for a short, beautiful coastal walk (**walk 53**).

Gruinard Bay is safe for swimming and has numerous sheltered pinky sand and shingle beaches along the otherwise rocky coastline, looking out to the Summer Isles and Gruinard Island. This island was infected with anthrax during infamous World War II experiments and was only recently freed of contamination. At the head of the bay, a recommended river walk begins (**walk 54**).

With fine coastal views throughout, the road now swings eastward to Little Loch Broom. This is one of the 'destitution roads'. During the potato famine of 1847 & 1848, Dowager Lady Mackenzie of Gairloch funded schemes to give many starving local men employment, easing their hardship considerably. At **Ardessie,** a spectacular roadside waterfall is just a foretaste of further delights upstream (**walk 55**). The hamlet of Dundonnell is dominated by the massive flanks of **An Teallach,** one of the finest mountains in Britain (**walk 56**). Near Dundonnell House, a single track road forks left for **Badrallach** (see **walk 57**).

The Dundonnell River drains Strath Beag between craggy hills in an entrancing series of falls and rapids, mostly visible from the road. A mile uphill of the Badrallach road junction however, the river plunges some 70 feet into an extremely narrow gorge, hidden from the carriageway (GR 123847). Heavily wooded with Scots pine, oak, rowan, hazel, alder, limes, beech and birch, the floor of the strath contrasts markedly with the bleak moorland beyond, overshadowed by the mighty peaks of An Teallach and the Fannichs. At the head of Strath More, a large lay-by with view indicator is worth a stop in clear weather for the prospect to Loch Broom.

STRATH MORE AND ULLAPOOL

At Braemore Junction, the A832 crosses a small ravine cut by the River Droma to meet the fast Inverness – Ullapool road. The gorge deepens abruptly in 500 yards. The Droma plunges in a dramatic 150 foot mares tail fall into **Corrieshalloch Gorge,** one mile long, 50 feet wide and nearly 200 feet deep. Formation began when meltwater from a huge glacier retreated back to the Dirrie Mor at the end of the last Ice Age, following natural major faults in the rock, the lines of least resistance. A beautiful mix of deciduous trees cling dizzily to the precipitous sides of the narrow chasm. An observation platform and bridge *(not recommended for vertigo sufferers)* are most easily reached by a short gentle path from a car park on the Ullapool road. An alternative path 0.6 mile from Braemore Junction on the A832, is much steeper, with some big steps which the less agile will find awkward.

The **River Cuileag** joins the Droma 0.5 mile upstream of Corrieshalloch. The Cuileag has formed an equally spectacular gorge with numerous falls along its length. Unlike its famous National Trust neighbour however, it is virtually unknown (see **walk 58**).

A short distance north of Braemore, the signed **Lael Forest Garden Trail** provides sheltered waymarked walking (**walk 59**). Three miles on at Inverlael, Gleann na Sguaib leads into the remote Beinn Dearg group of mountains, a real escapist's wilderness (**walk 60**). Three miles south of Ullapool, **Leckmelm's** 10 acre arboretum and Victorian walled garden were originally laid in the 1870's. Restored in the 1980s and opened to the public, the gardens boast a beautiful collection of trees and a wide range of azaleas and other shrubs.

The popular holiday resort of **Ullapool** lies on a raised beach projecting into attractive Loch Broom. The neat grid pattern streets were laid out in 1788 by the British Fishery Society. Many of the original herring fishermen's cottages still survive. Thanks to over fishing, the herring had disappeared by 1880. Fish stocks eventually recovered and once again it is a bustling fishing port. In recent decades, 'klondikers' have become a familiar sight, their huge rusting factory ships from Eastern Europe dwarfing the Cal Mac ferry to Stornaway. The sheltered loch also offers good sea angling for the amateur, notably for skate, cod, mackerel, haddock and whiting.

The innovative and award winning **Ullapool Museum** in West Argyle Street (*open all year, Mon-Sat*) expounds on local life over the last 200 years. The smaller **Loch Broom Museum,** in Quay Street houses artefacts from more recent times and geological specimens. Highland Stoneware in North Road provides a year round opportunity to visit a working pottery (*weekdays*, shop only on *Sat*). Other rainy day pursuits can be found at the Leisure Centre off Quay Street (swimming pool, fitness room, climbing wall & tennis). Weather permitting, three firms offer various day and part day local cruises, including around the seabird colonies of the Summer Isles. Motor and rowing boats can also be hired. In addition to regular services to Stornoway, Cal-Mac offer 'Across The Minch' *day cruises* and tours of Lewis. Mountain bikes are available for hire in West Argyle Street. Golfers are catered for with two courses. The smaller 9 hole Broomfield

Course, offers club hire. Hillwalkers can find numerous rewarding walks closeby, including **walk 61**. Full details of all activities can be obtained form the **Tourist Information Centre** in Argyle Street (*April – Nov*).

WALKING SECTIONS – EXPLANATORY NOTES

The walks are described in detail (unless the route is waymarked and obvious) and supported by accompanying maps where necessary. For the hillwalkers, the maps in the book are for illustrative purposes and are not intended to make the use of an Ordnance Survey map redundant. Heights reached in each walk are shown in both feet (ft) and metres (m) as most of us still think imperially, although the maps are now metric.

Gaelic is not an easy language to pronounce. To help you pronounce the hill you are climbing, a phonetic pronunciation is given in brackets after most mountain names. This can only be an approximation however, given that a number of Gaelic sounds are totally foreign to English, some names have been corrupted and regional variations in pronounciation exist.

Each major walk has an accompanying **FACT FILE** showing:

> **Total distance** of the walk in miles.

> Where the walk involves some climbing, the amount of **height gain** is shown both in feet & metres.
> The **time** given is an average time, including stops, in good summer conditions. Time taken may be *much longer* in adverse conditions or if terrain is snow covered.

> The **start** and **finish** points are given along with an **OS Sheet number.** This is for the relevant Ordnance Survey 1 50,000 sheet for that area, the most frequently used scale by walkers. All OS maps are drawn on a numbered grid of kilometre squares and 6 figure grid references (GR) are used.

> The **remarks** section highlights any potential difficulties of terrain under certain conditions.

Stalking season refers to any restriction during the deer stalking season. Stags are culled *1 July – 20 October* and hinds *21 October – 15 February*. Usually estates will allow access to the hills if no shooting is taking place. They often post local notices at access points regarding shooting but these may be missed, especially if you are an early riser. Estate contact phone numbers have been given where available. The onus is on the walker to check first. Tourist offices can also assist. The most critical time to check on access is from *mid-August to mid-October*, (this also includes the most critical time for grouse shooting). Most of the land is under private ownership and walkers who are considered trespassers can be required to leave that land. Reasonable force may be used to remove them. Freedom to roam the hills relies on the traditional mutual tolerance between landowners and the public. It is essential that walkers respect the necessary activities of the estates and do not interrupt the shooting. It should also be noted that it is an offence to camp or light fires on private land without the consent of the landowner. The estate contact numbers can be used to obtain such permission.

Dog owners should note that it is imperative to keep your dog under very close control at all times and on a lead when anywhere near sheep. During the **lambing period** (*April/May*), estates request that dogs are not taken through fields of sheep. Remember, a landowner is legally entitled to shoot any dog which is a threat to livestock.

Public transport if available is noted, including post buses. Tourist Information Centres can assist with timetables. Many of the walks, but not all, can be reached by limited public transport, and a private car is by far the most convenient mode of transport in the Highlands. Any likely parking problems are mentioned in the text of the walk. Please ensure that you do not block narrow roads, bearing in mind that farm vehicles and vehicles as large as Calor Gas tankers need to get through on the most minor of roads.

The Walks

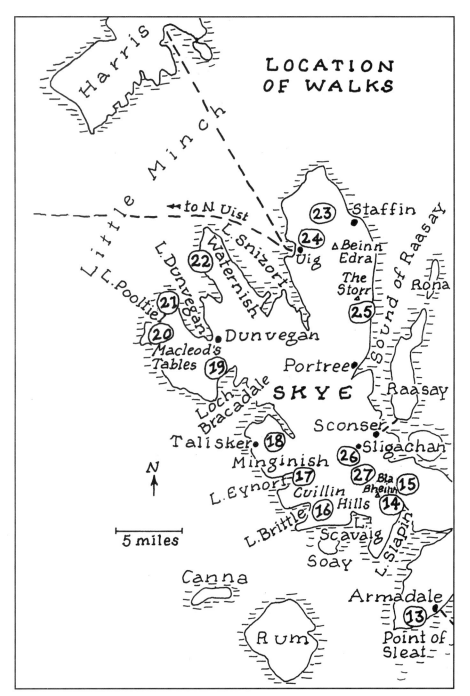

LOCATION OF WALKS

1 THE CREDIT CARD TRAVERSE – SGURR MOR TO SGURR NA CICHE

Have you ever looked at the attractive mountain scene on the Royal Bank of Scotland's Visa card and wonder from whence it was photographed? It shows the wild and complex ridges stretching from Sgurr Mor to Sgurr na Ciche, as seen from the shores of Loch Quoich. This two-day walk tackles this traverse of four Munros, undoubtedly one of the finest expeditions in the Highlands. The super fit could stagger round in one very long summer day or alternatively one could climb them in 2,3 or 4 separate, long, one day hikes. It is far more rewarding however to take one's time and enjoy a wild camp, high among these remote, rugged mountains. The going is quite rough at times with some easy scrambling and several potentially awkward river crossings. Some sections are also pathless, so this is not an outing for the inexperienced. Provided that there isn't a strong westerly wind blowing, an east to west traverse is recommended for the finer views.

Day 1 – From the road end at Loch Arkaig, follow the good track to Glendessary House. Just before the house, a stalkers' path begins, heading north to the pass at 360m, between Druim a' Chuirn and Fraoch Bheinn. The path is inclined to be boggy but easy to follow. Looking back, the peaks of Glen Dessary look dramatic when seen in early morning light, especially if still carrying some snow. Once onto the watershed, the path becomes indistinct and increasingly wet. There are several options for climbing **Sgurr Mor 3290ft/ 1003m** 'big peak' (skor moar). The first is shorter but involves a steep slog. Heading north from the watershed, descend through long grass and over the peat bog to reach the River Kingie. Provided that this is not in spate (which would dictate a long diversion upriver), you can paddle across then attack the steep, grassy pathless slopes leading directly to the col between Sgurr Mor and Sgurr an Fhuarain. A path then climbs the SE ridge to gain the small summit cairn.

The second option is longer but more pleasurable. From the watershed, swing round to the west and descend to the river. A short way above on the far bank, an excellent stalkers' path climbs steadily, dog-legging back to the col between An Eag and Sgurr Beag. This col is not easy to spot from below and the path is not obvious under snow, so careful navigation is required under winter conditions. Beyond the col, the path zigzags onto Sgurr Beag which is hidden behind several false summits. As height is gained, the views can be stupendous. Sgurr na Ciche looks particularly striking, its dramatic sharp cone rising symmetrically on all sides. Beinn Sgritheall, the rugged peaks of Knoydart, Loch Shiel, the Clunie hills, Torridon, Applecross and mountains south to Ben Nevis will also electrify the senses. Beyond the cairn, the narrow NE ridge drops to 750m. The fine path weaves between small rock outcrops, climbing steeply for 250m to the summit of Sgurr Mor.

The superb panoramas remain as you return to the col under An Eag; one of the joys of ridge walking. The going is now largely pathless and often quite narrow and rocky as An Eag is tackled, followed in turn by the Munro of **Sgurr nan Coireachan**, 'peak of the corries' (skoor nan korachan). From the Munro, the traverse continues WSW, dropping steeply on a grass and boulder ridge to the Bealach nan Gall. Where you choose to camp along the traverse is a personal decision. Given the roughness of the terrain, I preferred to use a bivvy bag rather than a tent. Not only lighter to carry, there is no difficulty finding a small grassy niche in which to tuck yourself near the col. Walkers with large tents may have to search around a bit and, if it is windy, may prefer to descend the grassy slopes south from the col and camp in the glen.

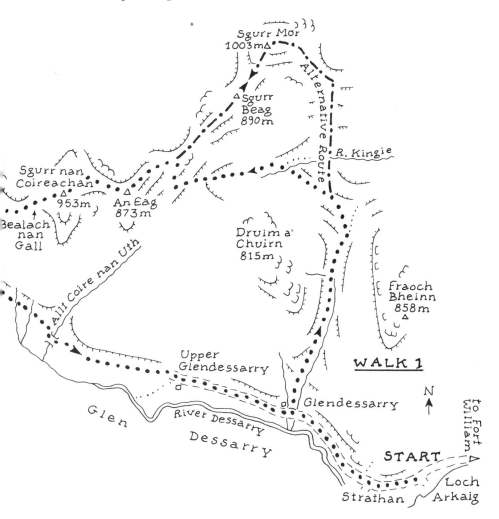

Day 2 – Navigationally, the next section is simple over **Garbh Chioch Beag** and the Munro, **Garbh Chioch Mhor** 3365ft / 1013m (garv cheech voar). The *'small'* and *'big rough paps'* are well named. A stone wall leads over an increasingly rocky ridge which require numerous small entertaining scrambles of up to grade 1 standard, depending on the chosen route. To the north lies slabby Coire nan Gall, into which a ragged, exhausted and hungry Bonnie Prince Charlie descended at night in his flight from Culloden; no mean achievement.

The wall ends just above the Feadan na Ciche, a narrow col which in high winds lives upto its name of Ciche's whistle or chanter. A path has developed onto **Sgurr na Ciche** 3410ft/ 1040m *'peak of the breast'* (skoor na keecha), hugging a grassy corridor well below the ridge crest on the south side. Just beyond a small pool, traces of path turn directly up towards the ridge, keeping to the right side of some bouldery scree. A short section beyond lacks a path and in mist it pays to build some temporary mini cairns in strategic positions, for later toppling. The ridge is gained just below the summit. When clear, the view is magnificent, particularly westward down Lochs Nevis and Hourn and across wild Knoydart.

Having regained the Feadan na Ciche, turn down the bouldery gully dropping SW. The gully is quite narrow, hemmed in by slabs and crags which can look enormous in mist. The rocks and grass provide a good clamber in places, requiring care, especially when wet. The route is a veritable botanic delight. Roseroot, white stonecrop, saxifrages, orchids, silverweed and tormentil cluster in the wet recesses while lady's mantle and thrift cling to the drier parts. About 300m / 985ft down, leave the gully and take the wide grassy terrace heading SE below the main crags of Garbh Chioch Mhor. Eventually you pick up a stream which can be followed down into the glen. Traces of a path ease progress though the long ankle twisting grass which is often wet and alive with bouncing frogs careering down the hillside. On joining the glen near the head of the Mam na Cloich Airde pass, the going is now straightforward if usually boggy, until Upper Glendessary House is reached. In spate conditions, the stream west of the Allt Coire nan Uth may necessitate a knee deep paddle. Fortunately the Alt Coire nan Uth itself has a bridge, tucked out of sight downhill of the path. However, bridges have a habit of disintegrating, so be prepared for a detour upstream after heavy rain. The track from Upper Glendessary will provide an easy finish to what should have been a memorable expedition.

FACT FILE
Distance: 22 miles Height gain: 7025ft/2140m
Time: 2 days
Start/ Finish: road end Loch Arkaig GR988916 OS Sheet 33 or 40
Remarks: In adverse weather and under snow, only for very experienced walkers.
Stalking season: Kingie Estate Stalker 01809 511261

EASY OPTIONS
From the road end near Strathan, easy tracks lead into Glen Pean and Glen Dessary affording pleasant valley walking. Pine martens can often be seen in the afforested areas.

2 INTO THE HEART OF KNOYDART

This two day walk (with one day options) ventures into the wild heart of Knoydart with optional ascents of two of the remotest Munros; **Ladhar Bheinn** 3348ft/1020m, (*larven*) one of the finest mountains in western Scotland and **Luinne Beinn** 3083ft/ 939m (*loonya vyn*). It is a serious undertaking with help a long way off should there be an accident. There are no bridges and rivers can rise quickly and become unfordable necessitating long detours. So be self-sufficient and check the long range weather forecast before you go. Do not be deterred however. The walk runs through one of the most remote, rugged and dramatically beautiful areas in Britain. Non-hillwalkers need not miss out. The first section to Barrisdale is easy and scenically magical. For the backpacker, doing the full round should provide an unforgettable wilderness experience.

From the car park at Kinloch Hourn, a well defined path heads west along the loch, hugging the steep hillside. The first mile passes through great clusters of rhododendrons, iris, birch and rowan, a picture in early summer. Wading birds are also likely to be well in evidence. The coastal views are stunning. Loch Hourn is narrow and the hills on the north side are very close; reminiscent of a Norwegian fjord. The path is a former important drove road and passes above Skiary House, once an inn. The old house at Runival used to be a schoolhouse and many ruins of former crofts dot the shore line. The ruined church at Barrisdale is yet another reminder of more populated days. Loch Hourn used to have a thriving herring fishing industry in the 18th century. Once this ceased, the agricultural life carried on much the same as it had done for centuries. Today only people connected with the estate are likely to face the harsh realities of life here.

Just 6.5 miles and three short climbs, lead to Barrisdale Bothy, standing in a beautiful, lonely setting, dominated to the west by Ladhar Bheinn and looking out to the Sound of Sleat. Beyond a short stretch of boggy ground, a stalkers' path zigzags up the grassy hillside on the lower slopes of Creag Bheithe before swinging round into cliff-girt Coire Dhorrcaill, a spectacular masterpiece in rock. The narrow path hugs the precipitous slopes above a deep gorge before reaching the river which can be crossed on boulders. Moderate, pathless, grassy slopes carpeted with orchids lead onto Druim a' Choire Odhair, a ridge of grass and avoidable small crags. Eventually a path develops and climbs steeply to a pointed top. Beyond, a short descent and reascent gains the narrow main ridge of Ladhar Bheinn which is followed westward to the summit; an outstanding viewpoint for the Knoydart Peninsula, Loch Hourn and the Hebrides. To vary the return to Barrisdale, one can follow the main ridge eastward over Aonach Sgoilte down to the Mam Barrisdale from where a path leads back down to the sea. This route is quite complicated and only recommended for strong walkers in clear conditions.

Having camped at Barrisdale or overnighted in the estate bothy (small charge), you have a choice. For those not wishing to climb Luinne Beinn, take the good path climbing a wooded slope and following the attractive Allt Gleann Unndalain up to the pass between Luinne Beinn and Sgurr a' Choire-bheithe. Munro baggers should head SW up the peaty (often wet) path banked by orchids and other bog lovers to the Mam Barrisdale pass. The route now becomes pathless and requires care in mist. From the col, steep grassy slopes wend between crags at the start of the long NW ridge of Luinne Beinn. The going eventually moderates over a series of rough knolls. The ridge steepens again for

the final 500 feet, made easier by traces of path. You are surrounded by some of the most rugged mountains in Britain. Seen close to, the slabby flanks of Meall Buidhe and Ben Aden look particularly intimidating. The eye is also drawn down Gleann an Dubh Lochain to Loch Nevis and to Loch Hourn. A short narrow crest leads to the east top. From here, the way down follows the initially narrow eastern ridge. The going is steep and occasionally slithery on the stonier sections.

At the foot of the ridge the two routes reunite. A fine path now zigzags down to the east and traverses along the foot of Druim Chosaidh to Lochan nam Breac. For anyone wishing to take an extra day, this would make a delectable camping site. Some poor stepping stones aid the crossing of the Allt Lochan na Cruadhach which flows into the eastern end of the lochan (in wet weather an awkward paddle). The path beyond leads to the regulating dam at the western end of Loch Quoich. Across the dam, the remains of an old road follows the north bank of the loch. This once served a shooting lodge and tenants housing at Kinlochquoich, submerged by the damming and raising of the loch.

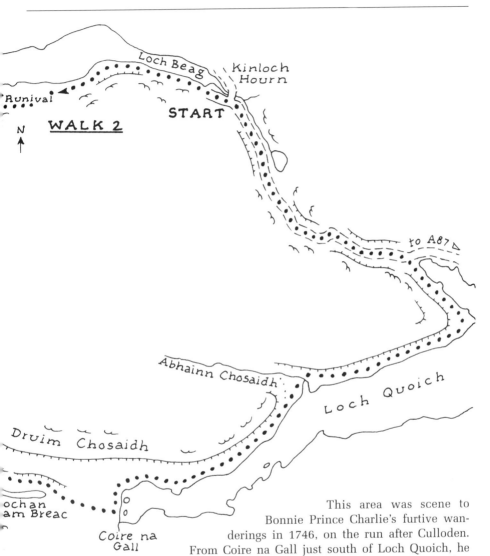

This area was scene to Bonnie Prince Charlie's furtive wanderings in 1746, on the run after Culloden. From Coire na Gall just south of Loch Quoich, he made his way at night onto Druim Cosaidh, slipping past sentries into Glen Cosaidh beyond. On another night he crept between four lines of troops to reach the head of Loch Hourn. Your journey will be much easier round to one of the most notorious rivers in Scotland; the Amhain Chosaidh. In extreme conditions it can swell to over 100 feet wide. Be prepared for long detours up the glen. Once across, 3 miles of mainly pathless heather and grass will see you to a foot bridge and the road (GR 986036). Rather than walk, you could leave a cycle in situ for the enjoyable 3 mile downhill run to Kinloch Hourn.

FACT FILE

Distance: 30 miles Height gain: 7220ft/2200m over 2 or 3 days (Ladhar Bheinn as a long day walk returning to Kinloch Hourn 19 miles plus 4500 ft) (Luinne Beinn as a day walk returning to Kinloch Hourn 19 miles plus 4100ft)
Start/Finish: Kinloch Hourn GR 952065 OS Sheet 33
Remarks: For camping other than at Barrisdale, obtain estate permission. Full expedition not recommended in wet weather.
Stalking season: end Aug – mid Oct, contact estate manager when at Barrisdale, if going off paths
Public Transport: Limited. Post bus operates late morning (Mon – Sat) Invergarry Post Office to Kinloch Hourn. Buses to Kyle pass through Invergarry.

EASY OPTIONS
As already intimated, the good track along Loch Hourn from Kinloch Hourn offers relatively easy walking and scenery of the very highest order. Mileage is optional: to Barrisdale and return is 13 miles and approximately 1000 feet of ascent.

A lso recommended is the gentle foreshore track on the north side of Loch Beag from Kinloch Hourn. There are an enormous variety of trees in the estate grounds. A previous owner must have been quite a collector. In June, masses of flowering rhododendrons mingle with the many shades of green, creating a lovely foreground to the surrounding craggy mountains.

3 ASCENT OF SGURR A' MHAORAICH 3370ft / 1027m

T ell your friends that you've scaled Sgurr a' Mhaoraich (skoor voereech) and undoubtedly you'll receive blank looks. The *'peak of the shellfish'* must rank as one of the least known mountains in Britain, yet deserves a place in the top 10 Munros for scenic splendour and interest of route. It stands in a commanding position above the eastern end of Loch Hourn, one of the most striking of all Highland lochs, nestling in truly wild country. Save this for a clear day when views will extend to the Inner and Outer Hebrides, Torridon, Ben Nevis and beyond. Sir Hugh Munro himself, the compiler of the Munro Tables, considered the summit panoramas as amongst the finest in the land.

T he twisting road to Kinloch Hourn crosses a bridge spanning a side branch of Loch Quoich. A small roadside cairn 550 yards to the SW, marks the start of a delightful, grassy stalkers' path climbing in easy zigzags onto Bac nan Canaichean. The splendid rugged peaks of Sgurr Mor, Gairich and pointed Sgurr na Ciche, draw the eye across Loch Quoich. Northward the scene is dominated by the grassy southern flanks of the South Shiel ridge, boasting seven Munros along its length. In June the route is lined with delicate white orchids and buzzards are likely to be seen above, floating lazily on warm thermals.

From Bac nan Canaichean, the ridge continues steeply though easily onto

Sgurr nan Eiricheallach. Beyond a short descent, lies a narrow and increasingly rocky and twisting ridge leading to the summit. Small remnants of dyke atop the ridge, seemingly without purpose. Presumably a wealthy landowner once built a substantial wall as a boundary marker. Some easy scrambling can be enjoyed (or avoided) on the narrower, rockier sections above the wild northern corries. One crag is actually pegged. The summit views can be truly breathtaking. Sgurr a' Mhaoraich Beag, 500m on, affords even greater views of Loch Hourn.

Easy descents can be made to Loch Quioch but denies you further scenic treats. Moderate grass and boulder slopes lead northward, before a steep drop to a rocky col at the head of the narrow corrie, Coire a' Chaorainn. A path of sorts aids progress. A steep, grassy climb, wending between wee crags gains the undulating ridge of Am Bathaich. The circular route of descent enables you to keep the fine view of Loch Hourn and Skye for some time. After a number of small ups and downs, the eastern end of the grassy ridge plunges abruptly to Glen Quoich. A stalkers' path can be picked up about 100ft down, zigzagging gently into the glen.

The path continues across, then follows the attractive Allt Coire a' Chaorainn, full of small, pretty cataracts, overlooked by banks of birch and rowan. The stream flows into the even more impressive River Quoich, with several fine waterfalls including one surrounded by rhododendrons, birch, oak and alder. In summer the floor of the woods are carpeted in chickweed wintergreen, a rather ugly name for a bonny flower. This river walk provides one of the highlights of the day. A virtually flat track leads along Glen Quoich to the road bridge and your start point. The going is dry underfoot but the boggy slopes are littered with orchids, butterwort, heath milkwort and starry saxifrage, providing a riot of colour in early summer.

FACT FILE
Distance: 7.5 miles Height gain 3200ft/ 968m
Time: 5 – 7 hours
Start/Finish: GR011034 OS Sheet 33

Remarks: Good paths on lower slopes, rough sometimes rocky ground elsewhere with a little easy, avoidable scrambling.
Public Transport: Postbus operates late morning, Mon- Sat between Invergarry Post Office & Kinloch Hourn
Stalking season: 1 Sept – 10 Oct Wester Glen Quoich Estate Tel 01809 511220

EASY OPTION
Follow the final 2.5 miles of the main walk above to the pretty River Quoich and Allt Coire a' Chaorainn, returning same way. Virtually flat and full of scenic and botanical interest.

4 THE FIVE SISTERS OF KINTAIL

B eloved by calendar photographers, the five most westerly peaks of the North Kintail Ridge are affectionately known as the Five Sisters and are very prominent when travelling east alongside Loch Duich. Only two are classified as Munros and can be climbed singly from Glen Shiel or together along with the second sister using the brutally steep and grassy western flanks. The complete traverse however, is one of the finest ridge walks in Scotland. A bike left at the end, or timing your walk to coincide with a bus, would save a 5 mile road walk at the finish.

There is no gradual way onto the ridge. The easiest ascent is by way of a peaty, eroded path that climbs steeply out of Glen Shiel from a wide gap between 2 forestry plantations, to reach the Bealach an Lapain, the col immediately west of Saileag. Once onto the ridge the gradient eases dramatically. Almost all of the traverse is along airy, twisting, narrow, grassy ridges littered with scattered rocks and wee crags. Viciously steep grassy slopes flank Glen Shiel whilst broken cliffs fall away to the north. Views are extensive throughout. I quickly lost count of the peaks I could name. *Happy memories flooding back of other idyllic mountain days.*

A long rocky ridge with innumerable knolls leads onto **Sgurr nan Spainteach** (skoor nan spaantyoch) *'the Spaniard's peak'*, so named because of the 300 Spanish soldiers who fought in the Battle of Glen Shiel in 1719 for the Jacobites against the Hanovarians and fled for their lives over this mountain. The going becomes quite rough and rocky down to the next col and onto **Sgurr na Ciste Duibhe** 1027m/3371ft (skoor na keeshtya doeya) *'peak of the dark chest'*, the first sister and Munro. From the massive summit cairn, there is an enchanting prospect of Loch Duich and beyond to Skye and the Outer Hebrides. The continuation to the pointed peak of **Sgurr na Carnach** (skoor na kaarnoch) *'rocky peak'*, is as rough as its name. It is easy to lose the path amongst the plethora of boulders. The summit is a fine perch from which to admire the precipitous crags beneath Sgurr nan Spainteach. The 600 foot ascent of *Sgurr Fhuaran* 1068m/3505ft (skoor oo aran), from the vee shaped gap of Bealach na Carnach can look rather daunting to tiring limbs but is easier than it looks. The path consists of steep, eroded earth and it is preferable to ignore it and boulder hop to the summit. This second Munro, *'the*

34

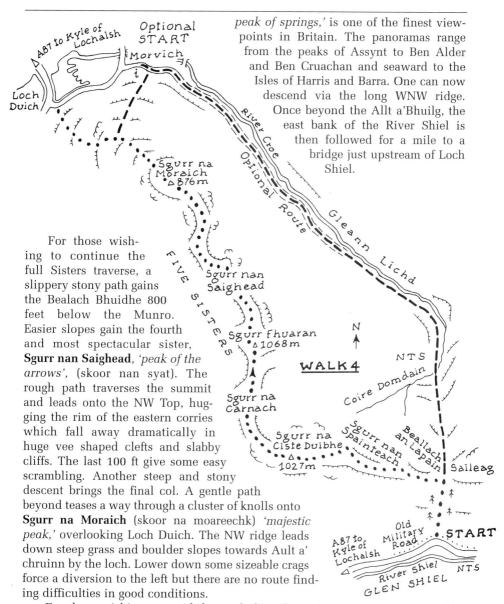

peak of springs,' is one of the finest viewpoints in Britain. The panoramas range from the peaks of Assynt to Ben Alder and Ben Cruachan and seaward to the Isles of Harris and Barra. One can now descend via the long WNW ridge. Once beyond the Allt a'Bhuilg, the east bank of the River Shiel is then followed for a mile to a bridge just upstream of Loch Shiel.

For those wishing to continue the full Sisters traverse, a slippery stony path gains the Bealach Bhuidhe 800 feet below the Munro. Easier slopes gain the fourth and most spectacular sister, **Sgurr nan Saighead**, *'peak of the arrows'*, (skoor nan syat). The rough path traverses the summit and leads onto the NW Top, hugging the rim of the eastern corries which fall away dramatically in huge vee shaped clefts and slabby cliffs. The last 100 ft give some easy scrambling. Another steep and stony descent brings the final col. A gentle path beyond teases a way through a cluster of knolls onto **Sgurr na Moraich** (skoor na moareechk) *'majestic peak,'* overlooking Loch Duich. The NW ridge leads down steep grass and boulder slopes towards Ault a' chruinn by the loch. Lower down some sizeable crags force a diversion to the left but there are no route finding difficulties in good conditions.

For those wishing to avoid the road altogether, a longer traverse is possible starting from Morvich. Park at the car park opposite the National Trust Centre and continue along the road for 0.5 mile. Go through a gate and follow the good track by the River Croe through Gleann Lichd to the foot of Coire Domdain. From here one can ascend directly to the aforementioned Bealach an Lapain. At the final sister, descend steeply and directly back to Morvich.

FACT FILE
Distance: 10.5 miles (plus 5 miles along road). Height gain: 5200ft/1584m
Time: 7 – 9 hours
Start: Glen Shiel GR 007135 Finish: GR 947205 OS Sheet 33
Remarks: Rough, narrow ridges not for the inexperienced under winter conditions
Stalking: No restrictions, NTS Property
Public Transport: buses from Kyle to Fort William and Inverness pass through Glen Shiel

EASY OPTION
Take the aforementioned track along Glen Lichd from Morvich for an easy and attractive valley walk.

5 ASCENT OF THE SADDLE 3317ft/1010m

The Saddle, rising above Loch Duich in lower Glen Shiel, is a complex majestic mountain of craggy deeply scoured corries and shapely narrow ridges and peaks. Its twin summits form a distinctive saddle shape when viewed from the glen. It deserves a top ten rating amongst Munros both as a superb viewpoint and for interest of ascent. On a clear day views extend to Ben Nevis and the Isles of Skye, Rum and Eigg across innumerable mountain ranges. The most interesting line of ascent is via the east, 'Forcan' ridge, which provides an exhilarating though easy (avoidable) scramble.

About half a mile east of the Achnangart quarry in Glen Shiel, an excellent stalkers' path begins and zig-zags gently up the grassy slopes to the col between Biod an Fhithich and Meallan Odhar from where the foot of the Forcan Ridge is easily gained. Initially steep and grassy, the ridge soon narrows to a rocky knife edged arete above the slabs of Coire Mhalagain. The rock strata are well tilted and appear to be the remains of an anticline. The entertaining scrambling along the crest is interspersed with walkable sections. All difficulties can be avoided by a path below the crest on the right hand side. I had to take my hat off in admiration for one middle aged gentleman I met. His walking gait was ungainly and required 2 sticks yet he managed the scrambling well. An inspiration to us all!

Beyond Sgurr nan Forcan, there is an unpleasant descent on very eroded slopes. It is preferable to scramble down the adjacent rock wall which is easier than it looks. The way continues easily over the east top before a steep eroded path leads to the airy summit cairn perched above a crag. A trig point lies 100 yards to the west along a grassy ridge.

Descend steep grassy slopes to the east then swing round to the Bealach Coire Mhalagain. *Munro baggers will probably wish to include the ascent of Sgurr na Sgine (skoor na skeenya). A steep slog from the col up grass and unstable boulders gains the NW top. A rocky ridge then leads SE over several small rises to the summit cairn; about 40 minutes from the col.*

From the Bealach Coire Mhalagain, descend beside the Allt Coire Mhalagain, an attractive sight even in relative drought conditions. Falls and water slides

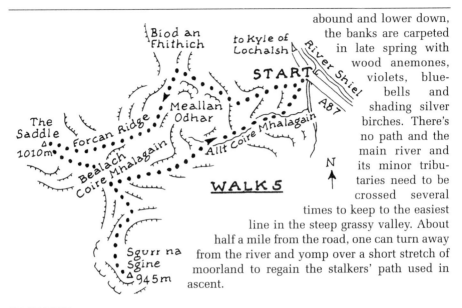

abound and lower down, the banks are carpeted in late spring with wood anemones, violets, bluebells and shading silver birches. There's no path and the main river and its minor tributaries need to be crossed several times to keep to the easiest line in the steep grassy valley. About half a mile from the road, one can turn away from the river and yomp over a short stretch of moorland to regain the stalkers' path used in ascent.

FACT FILE
Distance: 7 miles Height gain: 1000m/ 3382ft (with Sgurr na Sgine 9 miles & 1340m/4400ft)
Time: 6 hours
Start/Finish: Glen Shiel GR 968143 OS Sheet 33
Remarks: Forcan Ridge difficult under winter conditions, only for the highly experienced
Stalking season: Glenshiel Estate Manager tel. 01599 511282
Public Transport: Fort William – Kyle of Lochalsh and Inverness – Kyle buses pass through Glen Shiel

6 THE ASCENT OF BEINN FHADA 3385ft / 1032m & A' GHLAS BHEINN 3006ft / 918m

B einn Fhada or Ben Attow (*byn atta*) means '*long mountain*', a simple description of one of the western Highlands most complex and interesting mountains. To the south it presents steep grassy flanks stretching for 7 miles, to the north, wild corries. Its summit is part of a large plateau which to the west tapers to airy rocky ridges. This walk samples each aspect of its character in a superb scenic outing. For the energetic Munro bagger, it can be easily combined with neighbouring A'Ghlas Bheinn (*a glashven*), which allows a greater appreciation of Beinn Fhada's magnificent north side.

L eave the A87 at the head of Loch Duich and follow the minor road which ends at a forestry car park at Dorusduain in Strath Croe. For those just climbing Beinn Fhada, take the track towards Dorusduain House then descend the path to a

bridge over the Abhainn Chonaig. A good stalkers' path heads up Gleann Choinneachan, an impressive steep sided valley of tumbling streams overlooked by the small crags and deeply incised gullies of A' Ghlas Bheinn and the craggy majestic northern corries of Beinn Fhada. Nearer at hand a colourful selection of flora can be found including some fairly rare orchids. *(Those looking for a relatively easy walk would enjoy this section).*

About 1000 yards below the Bealach an Sgairne, a cairn on the right indicates the start of an excellent path which climbs easily into Coire an Sgairne and zigzags onto the edge of Beinn Fhada's plateau about a mile south of Meall a' Bhealaich. Exceedingly gentle grassy slopes (needing accurate navigation in mist) leads SE to the summit cairn. On a clear day the wonderful vistas extend from Ben Nevis to Torridon and seaward to the Inner and Outer Hebrides. Not for nothing did my chant the day I climbed these hills become, 'Praise the Lord and grab the camera!'

The most exciting descent route returns back across the plateau to the southern rim of Coire an Sgairne and onto a rounded top (GR 990196). Beyond, the route becomes rocky and narrow with airy ridges rimming the dramatic Coire Gorm and Coire Chaoil. Some scrambling is involved. It is not technically difficult but requires care and can be tricky if wet. From Sgurr a'Choire

Ghairbh, descend the steep ridge swinging round to Beinn Bhuidhe then continue NW down very steep grassy slopes, weaving between the rocky outcrops to Dorusduain. For those with jippy knees or if the ground is wet, it is safer to descend the easier slopes west from Beinn Bhuidhe and pick up the path above the Abhainn Chonaig back to Dorusduain.

For walkers including the ascent of A' Ghlas Bheinn, take the signed Falls of Glomach track northward from Dorusduain for 0.75 mile to the end of the forest. Strike up the steep grassy slopes onto the broad WNW ridge of the mountain. The ridge becomes more bouldery and better defined with height. Beautiful views accompany you throughout, particularly to seaward.

Descend the south ridge to the Bealach an Sgairne, a long and complex series of rocky knolls requiring frequent detours, interwoven with grassy corridors (confusing in mist). By always moving to the east around any obstruction, one can keep to grass and avoid any difficulties. From the col it is possible to climb directly up the gully ahead onto Beinn Fhada – not recommended! It is very steep and eroded and requires awkward scrambling and a strong sense of adventure. Instead zigzag up the steep grassy slopes to the east of the gully, working a way between the crags onto Meall a' Bhealaich and follow the hummocky ridge up to the plateau. Alternatively, a longer though easier way would be to descend Gleann Choinneachain for 1000 yards and pick up the previously described path ascending into Coire an Sgairne. The route is then as per Beinn Fhada above.

FACT FILE
Distance: Beinn Fhada 8 miles, Height gain: 3750ft/1140m (with A' Ghlas Bheinn, 10 miles 5382ft/1640m)
Time: 6 – 9 hours
Start/Finish: Dorusduain, Strath Croe GR 981223 OS Sheet 33
Remarks: Beinn Fhada difficult under winter conditions, not for the inexperienced. Accurate navigation essential in hillfog.
Public Transport: Kyle of Lochalsh – Fort William & Inverness buses only as far as Loch Duich
Stalking: Beinn Fhada no restrictions NTS property. A'Ghlas Bheinn contact Inverinate estate manager tel 01599 511303 / 250.

EASY OPTIONS
1 – The aforementioned path up **Gleann Choinneachain** from Dorusduain
2 – **Ratagan Forest Walk** Begin at the Ratagan Youth Hostel on the south shore of Loch Duich. Head back along the road towards the village. Beyond the houses, turn right onto a gently climbing forest track. Follow this, enjoying the views over the loch to Beinn Fhada and the Five Sisters. Walk quietly and you'll spot a variety of birds and with luck a pine marten which thrive here. After about 2.5 miles, the track swings right and descends to the road. This is then followed back to the start.
3.75miles, approx. 100m/ 328ft of ascent, 1.5 hours

7 THE FALLS OF GLOMACH

F or connoisseurs of waterfalls, this full day hike is a must; these falls being arguably the finest in Scotland and certainly one of the longest. The Allt a' Ghlomaich, *'the burn of the chasm'*, flows from a large basin holding three lochans so that even in relative drought conditions, the falls remain impressive. The walk can be extended to include the neighbouring Falls of Carnach, which lie in a similar setting but, unlike their neighbour, can be seen in their entirety.

T he most interesting approach is along Glen Elchaig, a bonny, partially wooded glen with numerous craggy hills overlooking the broad river. From Loch Duich, take the single track road along the western shore of Loch Long. The public road ends 6 miles beyond Ardelve. The rough road continuing along Glen Elchaig makes for very easy walking or cycling. Three miles along, a fine small double waterfall thunders through a gorge of tilted rock strata. In a further 2 miles a bridge crosses the River Elchaig at the foot of a dramatic deep cut gorge, a mile in length. Railway sleepers cross the worst of the bog. A narrow, muddy path now climbs into the jaws of the gorge, hugging the steep, grassy hillsides which are carpeted in bluebells, wood anemones and orchids. Far below, the Allt a' Ghlomach cascades in a series of small falls. The occasional easy, though careful, scramble is required. *It is not a place for vertigo sufferers.*

The walk culminates at the head of the gorge with the sight of the Falls of Glomach plunging some 300 feet. A small upper fall turns a corner then leaps 80 feet before dividing into two at the top of a rock buttress. Approximately 50 feet of the lower fall cannot be seen. For the best views, a path requiring care, descends about a third of the height of the falls.

For those wishing to extend the walk to the Falls of Carnach, cross the river (when safe) above the falls and head eastward over the moorland for about 0.5 mile before swinging NE under the gentle slopes of Meall Sguman, to pick up a stalkers' path descending to Carnach in Glen Elchaig via Loch Lon Mhurchaidh. This cuts down the steep hillside above the falls which are found at GR 032273. They comprise four closely linked falls in a grassy bowl. The top cascade of some 7ft is followed by two waterslides approximately 50ft in length which lead in turn to a final plunge of 66ft. The path continues down the hanging valley to Carnach and the good track in Glen Elchaig.

A shorter, though more strenuous and less picturesque route to the Falls of Glomach, begins at Dorusduain in Strath Croe, reached by a minor road from the causeway across Loch Duich. A signed path from the forestry car park ascends NW through coniferous forest before more open ground above the Allt an Leold Ghainearn-bhalch leads to the Bealach na Sroine. From the narrow pass, the path crosses gentle moorland for some distance. A short, steeper descent then gains the top of the falls. Return the same way.

FACT FILE

Distance: via Glen Elchaig 12 miles (10 miles can be cycled). Height gain: 800ft/244m

(With Falls of Carnach: 15 miles, 985ft/ 300m)

Time: 6 – 8 hours

Falls of Glomach via Doruisduain: 8 miles, 2133ft/ 650m, 5 hours

Start/Finish: Glen Elchaig GR 949298 OS Sheet 33 or Doruisduain GR 981223

Stalking: usually no restrictions but check local notices

Public Transport: none Glen Elchaig. Buses to Kyle pass along Loch Duich, 2 miles from Doruisduain

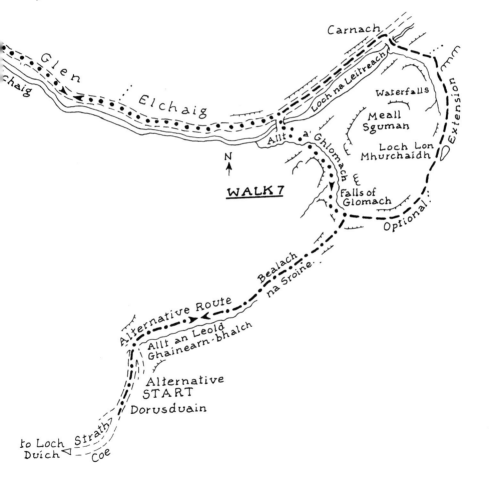

8 GLENELG–ARDINTOUL CIRCULAR

This scenically varied circular walk explores some of the unfrequented coast and moorland to the south of Loch Alsh. Apart from the second mile which is inclined to be wet and boggy, it is mainly on good paths and tracks. Being largely sheltered, it makes an ideal outing on a day of high winds. There is an optional short ascent to the viewpoint of Glas Bheinn 394m/ 1292ft.

Park in the large car park just above the Kylerhea ferry jetty, north of Glenelg village and take the signed track for 'Ardintoul & Totaig'. As the track ascends gently into a small coniferous plantation there are good views behind along the Sound of Sleat, with a strong chance of seeing seals. At a junction of tracks approaching a line of pylons, bear left into scattered deciduous woodland. The track ends at a pylon. Beyond, a narrowing, occasionally muddy path leads into denser woodland clinging to slopes plunging abruptly to the sea below. In spring, bluebells, violets, primroses and lousewort proliferate. After crossing a second deeply incised stream, fork right at a junction alongside a fence. On reaching the western point of the sandy bay of Camas nan Gall, Garbhan Coasach, cross the fence and take a much improved path descending gently to the shore. As the bay is then followed towards Ardintoul, the views of Kyle Rhea give way to those across Loch Alsh. The hillsides around Balmacara are smothered in a blazing yellow carpet of gorse, overlooked by the Applecross hills.

Approaching Ardintoul, the route follows a wall, then cuts across a field. Continue left towards some trees by the shore, then beyond a large house, turn right onto a forest road climbing inland. Apart from one short steep section, the gradient is gradual to the pass, Bealach Luachrach. Views extend across Glenelg

Bay and down the Sound of Sleat, to Loch Long, the Shiel hills and the rugged mountains south of Gleann Beag. For even finer vistas, leave the track at the pass and follow the remains of a fence NW to the trig point on Glas Bheinn, perched airily above craggy western flanks. Having returned to the pass, continue along the track descending westward into afforested Glen Bernera. This leads to the road about one mile east of the start point.

FACT FILE
Distance: 8.5 miles Height gain: 950ft/289m Time 4 – 5 hours
(with Glas Bheinn 9.5 miles, 1455ft/ 443m, 5 – 6 hours)
Start/ Finish: Road end north of Glenelg GR 795214 OS Sheet 33

9 GLEANN BEAG

This easy walk along a good track, explores an attractive glen full of historic interest. Gleann Beag lies half a mile south of Glenelg off the road to Arnisdale. Park up two miles along the narrow road into the glen and take time to visit the Iron Age Brochs of Dun Telve and Dun Trodden, some 2000 years old, the finest examples of such structures on mainland Scotland. Stairs spiral up between the inner and outer stone walls which were once around 50 feet high and roofless. Only a section 33 feet high remains at Dun Telve, as much was taken for local building until conservationists stepped in. Archaeologists believe that there were once one or two raised platforms in the centre, covered by a thatched roof with a large central area for light and a fire. Probably only a temporary residence in times of danger, the people most likely lived within this central section rather than in the cramped and dark galleries between the walls.

Either drive or walk up to the road end at Balvraid a mile beyond the brochs. There is limited parking for three or four cars. Ensure that farm access is kept clear. Continue up the glen through the grazing land, on the track past the farm. At the top of a rise in about half a mile, the remains of a fort lie on the right, perched above a precipitous gorge. Dun Grugaig is even older than the brochs. Unfortunately only the base wall survives. It was larger than the brochs and semicircular with the gorge defending the open side. Closeby, traces can be found of another ancient stone and earthwork construction.

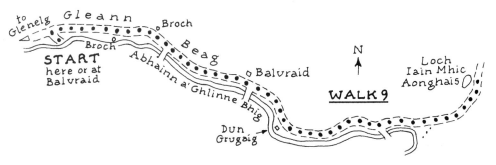

43

The track continues just above the wide river which is often fringed with pretty deciduous woodland and overlooked by the craggy flanks of Beinn Chapuill and Beinn Sgritheall. About 2.5 miles from Balvraid, lies the small lochan, Loch Iain Mhic Aonghois, named after a local, John MacInnes. Gaelic legend tells of a waterhorse which lived under the water and possessed magical powers. MacInnes foolishly tried to use it to plough his fields. The horse turned on him and threw him into the loch where he was drowned.

Retrace your steps from the loch.

FACT FILE

Distance: 5 miles if starting from Balvraid, approximately 360ft/ 110m height gain, allow 3 – 3.5 hours with the brochs

10 ASCENT OF BEINN SGRITHEALL 974m/3164ft

'*Scree or gravel hill*' (screehal) sweeps up from the northern shore of Loch Hourn like a precipitous scree draped ridge tent. It is possible to climb it however without encountering any scree by way of the west ridge. As a viewpoint, the peak is outstanding. Sir Hugh Munro considered the views as some of the most beautiful in Scotland and who am I to argue with the great man! I was so taken with the mountain that I named my next house 'Sgritheall'.

About 1 mile NW of Arnisdale, just above the north shore of Loch Hourn, an old right of way to Glenelg begins. The path is very indistinct and if you lose it, just continue up the steep broken slopes into a band of scattered deciduous trees which perfectly frame the Knoydart mountains across the loch. With the exception of Ben Lawers, I have never seen such a delectable profusion of flowers on a Scottish mountain. The lower slopes are carpeted in bluebells, pale heath bugle, primroses, wood anemones, greater stitchwort, violets, butterwort, oxalis, globeflowers, speedwell, avens, a variety of orchids, milkwort and creeping cinquefoil to name but a few.

The path becomes better defined in the woodland and wends up through small crags to the top of the escarpment. It again fizzles out on reaching the long west ridge though occasionally reappears and is obvious on the upper slopes. In clear conditions the route is straightforward with eye catching vistas throughout across Loch Hourn to rugged Knoydart, the Shiel hills and to Rum, Eigg and Skye beyond the Sound of Sleat. Predominantly easy grassy slopes become increasingly stony and steepen for the final climb, wending in between wee crags. There are no difficulties however, making me wonder why most walkers labour up the awful scree slopes from Arnisdale. The airy summit is dramatically

44

perched above broken cliffs and screes plunging brutally for over 3000 feet, directly to Loch Hourn; a grand eagle's eerie.

It is best to retrace your steps in descent. If a circular route is preferred, head eastward to a minor top then descend to Arnisdale via the Bealach Arnasdail on a bouldery and scree riddled route.

FACT FILE
Distance: 4 miles Height gain: 3200ft/ 975m
Time: 4 – 5 hours
Start/Finish: minor road west of Arnisdale GR 825117 OS Sheet 33
Stalking season: Eilanreach Estate Manager 01599 522244
Public Transport: once daily post bus Kyle – Arnisdale passes the start

EASY OPTION – see coastal path walk from Corran **walk 11B**

11 WALKS FROM CORRAN

The tiny isolated hamlet of Corran lies at the end of the tortuous but scenic road following the north shore of Loch Hourn. From the car park at the road end, several fine routes are possible catering for all abilities.

11A – GLEN ARNISDALE CIRCULAR

This route is suitable for hillwalkers looking for an easier day away from the high tops, venturing through a wild, crowd-free region amidst craggy hills and picturesque rivers and lochans. Choose a clear day, preferably not just after heavy rain to avoid problems in crossing the burns.

From Corran take the path signed 'Kinloch Hourn' which heads inland over grazing land into the rough and deep-cut Glen Arnisdale, following the south bank of the wide river under the broken cliffs of Druim Fada. As you progress up the glen, a fine prospect opens up westward to the Cuillins of Skye. Beyond some woodland and a waterfall, the narrowing path crosses the river and reaches the Dubh-Lochain. The path continues along the north shore of the two lochans. The marching line of pylons are an unwelcome intrusion into an otherwise attractive glen. Bear left onto a path that passes close to two ruined crofts and follows the line of pylons and the Allt an Tomain Odhair. In half a mile the main path turns northwards away from the river. Leave it and take to an indistinct path still following the line of the stream and pylons. In a further mile, bear left onto a path climbing westward over a low pass before descending into Coire Chorsalain beneath cliff-girt Beinn Clachach and Beinn nan Caorach. From the gentle upper glen, the path zig zags down steep slopes past a wooded gorge and waterfall to reach the fields beside the River Arnisdale. There are enchanting views over Corran and Loch Hourn to the rugged Knoydart mountains. Having crossed the river bridge, the outward route is rejoined for the final 0.75 mile.
Distance: 8 miles Height gain: 420m/ 1378ft Time: 5 hours

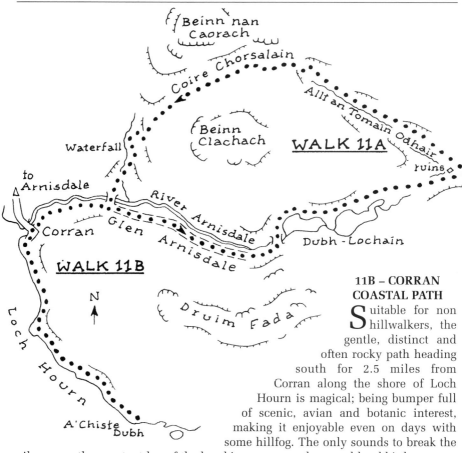

11B – CORRAN COASTAL PATH

Suitable for non hillwalkers, the gentle, distinct and often rocky path heading south for 2.5 miles from Corran along the shore of Loch Hourn is magical; being bumper full of scenic, avian and botanic interest, making it enjoyable even on days with some hillfog. The only sounds to break the silence are the constant lap of the breaking waves onshore and loud birdsong.

From the road end, the signed, 'Coastal path' initially follows above the stony beach. About 100 yards beyond a ramshackle hut, the path climbs a short way into pretty deciduous woodland and thereafter alternates between the shore and just above the rocky points. The views are superb throughout. Across the loch, the huge, complex and cliff-girt massif of Ladhar Bheinn, is particularly striking, whilst to the north, Beinn Sgritheall dominates. The Red Cuillin and Blaven on Skye show well beyond the Sound of Sleat. An abundance of primroses narrowly outnumber the violets and flags making it particularly pretty in late spring. Binoculars are highly recommended. Otters frequent these waters. I also identified over 20 different kinds of birds ranging from grey herons, oystercatchers, sand-pipers, redstart and a lone eagle circling high above rocky Druim Fada. The path ends at a point looking out over three tiny islets to Barrisdale Bay and the magnif-icent cliffs of Coire Dhorcail beneath Ladhar Bheinn. Retrace your steps to Corran. *Distance: 5 miles Height gain: negligible Time: 2.5 – 3 hours*

12 KYLERHEA COAST

This short, scenic coastal outing on the quiet east coast of Skye provides an excellent opportunity for spotting otters, in addition to seals, plentiful here. Hillwalkers can consider an optional climb of Ben Aslak 610m / 2002ft (GR 751191), a fine viewpoint.

Park in the lay-by (opposite the road to the Otter Haven) 300 yards west of the junction of the Broadford road and the lane leading down into the hamlet of Kylerhea, a short distance south of the Glenelg-Kylerhea ferry pier. Walk down the lane into the hamlet, past the scattered crofts and fields following the signed 'Footpath to Kinloch'. This bears off left from the main track to a bridge over the gushing Kylerhea River whose banks and surrounds are carpeted in globe flowers, marsh marigolds and bluebells. The official path (to Kinloch) forks right at a junction, 50 yards beyond the bridge and keeps to the right of a fence. It is usually very wet underfoot however and it is better to take the left fork over the grass passing two ruins to reach the shore of the picturesque bay of Bagh Dun an Ruadh. This is a great place for beachcombing and for spying seals and otters: look for the tell-tale V-shape wake otters create when swimming. Work your way along the beach to the trees then ascend just above the shore. You can walk straight uphill at any time to join the official footpath which rises to several hundred feet above the loch. Be warned however, it is often a running stream and it is usually better to make

your own way over the moorland closer to the shore, unless you are visiting during a drought period. Flowers flourish on the surrounding slopes, particularly lousewort, milkwort, violets, orchids and bog asphodel. Scenically it is worthwhile venturing one to two miles along the coast from Kylerhea for the extensive views along the Sound of Sleat and across to the mainland hills.

In clear weather, hillwalkers can extend the walk by ascending the long but straightforward rough moorland forming the ENE ridge of Ben Aslak, to gain the twin topped summit ridge above the precipitous northern flanks. The result of your labours are far reaching vistas across Skye, the Shiel hills and down the Sound of Sleat to Knoydart. It is easiest to retrace your steps in descent although a circular walk is possible. Head SW from the summit for a short way until breaks in the craggy ground allow you to descend NW towards the minor outlying top of Beinn Bheag. Then descend the moorland to the Broadford road near the head of the pass and follow the quiet road back down towards Kylerhea.

FACT FILE
Distance Optional, 2 – 4 miles recommended, allow 1 – 2 hours. (Ben Aslak 7 miles, 640m/2100ft ascent, 5 hours)
Start/ Finish: Kylerhea GR 787208 OS Sheet 33
Remarks: The walk along to the first bay is easy and good underfoot, boots essential thereafter. If you fail to spy otters during the walk, visit the hide at the Otter Haven above the hamlet, you may have more luck.
Stalking season: Check locally if climbing Ben Aslak
Public Transport: Kylerhea – Glenelg car ferry runs frequently April – October

13 POINT OF SLEAT

This walk explores the wild moorland and attractive coast at the tip of the Sleat Peninsula in southern Skye; in complete contrast to the verdant ground just to the north. An easy track for much of the way, eventually narrows to a boggier path. There is an entrancing seaward prospect from many points along the route. Rum, Eigg, Ardnamurchan, Tiree, the Uists and the mountains of Morar and Moidart are all prominent. Several delightful coves and bays are passed; ideal picnic grounds.

There is limited parking at the road end by the old church in Aird of Sleat. Beyond a gate, a good track undulates easily over heather and rocky moor. The verges are a colourful profusion of lousewort, campion, ransoms, yellow cats ear, orchids, milkwort, thyme and tormentil, to name but a few. Dwarf rose hips struggle to rise above the heather; an indication of the salt laden high winds which prevail. Numerous ruined crofts are passed. A sad reminder of the Highland Clearances when landowners considered the profit from sheep was more important than their tenants livelihoods.

After 1.5 miles, the track narrows beside an entertaining stream with a double waterfall. Having crossed a third footbridge over the stream and passed through two gates, you can see down to a tiny harbour. A short detour can be made to the right, down to the harbour. From here, continue westward, scrambling easily onto Acairseid an Rubha. The triple cairned highpoint of this headland is a superb viewpoint for the Inner Hebrides and across the sound to the Cuillins. Retrace your steps until just before the last footbridge, then turn right. The path deteriorates and is not always clear. Climb the initially rocky, then more heathery slopes, keeping

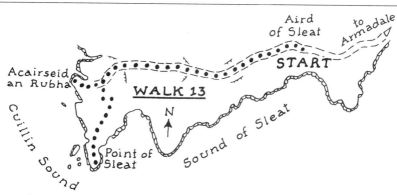

close to the fence on the left. At a corner in the fence, the path keeps straight on before turning briefly eastward over hillocks and through a small marshy dip. Turning south once more, it climbs easily uphill to the left of a large knoll. Over the top of a marshy rise, a good path reappears and descends to a small bay and the lighthouse. From a further small rise beyond, the far reaching vistas extend to the mountains of Lochaber and the Outer Hebrides. Camas Daraich is the enchanting bay to the east; usually a hive of seabird activity, including shags, gannets and kittiwakes. Otters too, frequent the coast. Retrace your steps. *No hardship in such splendid surroundings.*
6 miles, 4 hours, approximately 900ft/ 274m of ascent

This walk can be combined with a visit to the **Clan Donald Visitor Centre**, a museum of Gaelic history (*daily April – Oct*) some 4 miles to the north east. There are also 40 acres of gardens surrounding the ruins of the 19th century Armadale Castle.

14 THE ASCENT OF BLAVEN 3044ft/ 928m

B laven, or more correctly, Bla Bheinn (blaavyn) 'blue mountain', is the only Munro on Skye which is not part of the main Cuillin ridge. It is a majestic, isolated, cliff-girt mountain in its own right and an excellent vantage point for the Red and Black Cuillin and the mainland. Its ascent in good weather is a relatively straightforward hillwalk, though is rough and stony underfoot in the upper reaches. As with all Skye mountains, it should not be undertaken lightly in poor conditions. When seen across Loch Slapin from Torrin, Blaven is one of the great sights of the Highlands, with its numerous tops, huge spread of eastern cliffs and massive gullies. The route allows for a close inspection of this rock spectacular.

P ark at the bridge over the Allt na Dunaiche, half a mile south of the head of Loch Slapin. The initially peaty path is rather boggy after rain. In compensation, it follows the north bank of the entertaining river. This has cut a pretty birch lined gorge, full of small falls and dark pools, fronting Blaven's mighty cliffs. The gentle heather moorland gives way to fairly steep and stony slopes leading up into Coire Uaigneich. A huge erratic boulder lies in the heart of the grassy corrie bowl.

Bla
Bheinn (Blaven)
△928m

START

N

Allt na Dunaiche

WALK 14

Leaving the tourist route for the return, take a steep path in the scree at the head of the corrie (some cairns) heading westward to the dip under the South Top with a tiny lochan. From the dip, a mixture of simple scrambling and slithering up a loose stony path NE, gains the Top. From here to the main summit, you should hopefully be treated to breathtaking views to Applecross, Knoydart and Kintail and across the deep valley of Srath na Creitheach to the main Cuillin ridge. Be warned however, Skye clouds can act in a most peculiar fashion. Although I climbed Blaven on a sunny day, a huge wedge of cloud kept billowing in from the north and rushing up the Srath na Creitheach. The Black Cuillin remained clear of cloud but I only caught one fleeting glimpse.

A short, narrow, rocky arrete connects the South Top and spacious summit dome. Scramblers can make the easy though slightly airy scramble along a ledge leading to a dip in the ridge. The less adventurous can take an earth gully a short way down to the right, to just below the dip.

Descend the east ridge from the summit using a clear and well cairned path. There is some grass but generally it is stony and loose, requiring careful footwork. En route, there are some spectacular views to the mountain's complex array of slab-by buttresses and gullies. Below 2000 feet, the terrain becomes increasingly grassy underfoot. The path, now less distinct, zig zags down to the left of a vertical gully and huge cliffs. Once back into Coire Uaigneich, the path of ascent can be rejoined on the north west side of the stream.

FACT FILE

Distance: 4.5 miles with 3100 ft / 944m of ascent

Time: 4 – 5 hours

Start/ Finish: Loch Slapin on Broadford – Elgol road GR 562217 OS Sheet 32

Remarks: Not recommended to inexperienced walkers in hillfog or under snow

Stalking season: Strathaird Estate tel. 01471 866260

Public Transport: twice daily postbus (Mon – Fri) Broadford – Elgol, passes start

15 CAMASUNARY WALKS (SKYE)

The hilly Strathard Peninsula just north of Elgol, offers a range of walking options catering for all levels of ability and inclination. All routes encompass part of the stunning coastline fringing Loch Scavaig and enjoy some of the finest views of the Cuillin mountains to be found on Skye.

A – Kilmarie – Camasunary The easiest walk in the area follows a track which leaves the A881 road to Elgol about 500 yards south of Kilmarie (GR545173). It ascends relatively gently across moorland to the broad pass of Am Mam. A dramatic prospect is suddenly revealed, encompassing the white washed buildings of Camasunary behind the delightful sandy bay of Camas Fhionairigh and Loch Scavaig bordered by the savage Cuillins. The distant islands of South Uist, Barra and the Small Isles complete a wonderful picture. The track continues in steep zig zags down to the grass fringed beach, a great spot for a picnic. Return the same way.
5 miles with 330m / 1082ft of ascent, allow 2.5 hours.

B – Camasunary and Ben Meabost 346m / 1135ft This relatively short but fairly rough and energetic minor hill and coastal route affords breathtaking vistas of mountain and seascape. Take the track from Kilmarie to Camasunary as above. Now turn south along the coastal path which climbs onto low cliffs and often hugs the cliff edges above Loch Scavaig. Having traversed below Beinn Leacach, it drops quite steeply to the rocky bay at the entrance to Glen Scaladal. (Note that this section from Camasunary can be very muddy & slippery in or after heavy rain and in such conditions it may be advisable to make your own way over the moorland tops of Beinn Leacach using the sheep tracks to advantage).

Cross the main stream issuing from Glen Scaladal and follow its tributary stream east and SE, climbing the steep moorland slopes to gain the broad col between Ben Cleat and Ben Meabost. An easy climb up the broad west flanks brings the summit of Ben Meabost, a superb viewpoint for Loch Slapin and the Sleat Peninsula and across Loch Scavaig to the Cuillin. Head NNW from the cairn, descending the steepening slopes to meet the 'Am Mam' track about 0.5 mile from the start. Some rocky ground and small outcrops have to be circumnavigated. Alternatively, some walkers may prefer (or should hillfog suddenly descend) to return to the col and descend the easy slopes SE to join the Elgol road 1.5 miles from the start.
6.5 miles, 530m/ 1739ft of ascent, 4 – 5 hours

C – An easier variant on route **2** would be to avoid Ben Meabost and continue along the coastal path from Glen Scaladal to Elgol, enjoying the continuing fine views over Loch Scavaig. From the bay, the path again climbs above low cliffs, often hugging the edge of cliffs dropping sheer to the sea. Willow and birch cling tenaciously to the precipitous slopes, alive with orchids and other colourful flora. The path finishes by the houses high above Elgol jetty. To avoid a 3 mile road walk back to Kilmarie, catch the *mid afternoon* post bus (*Mon – Fri*). Alternatively, follow the minor road from Elgol to Glasnakille and take the scenic track and path high above Loch Slapin leading to Kilmarie.
6 or 9 miles, 330m / 1082ft of ascent, 3.5 – 5 hours (via Glasnakille 10 miles, allow 6 hrs)

D – Ascent of Sgurr na Stri 497m / 1631ft For the more adventurous hillwalker, the ascent of this lowly rocky peak offers an exhilarating expedition and exceptional views of the Cuillins and surrounding lochs. 'Peak of strife' derives from a point-

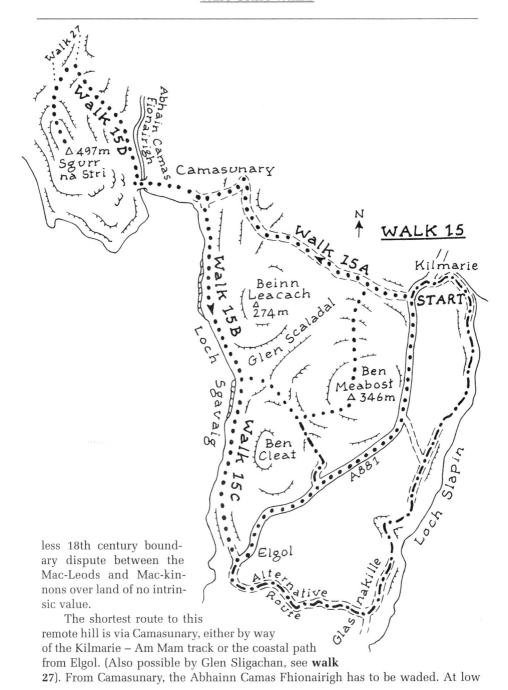

less 18th century bound-
ary dispute between the
Mac-Leods and Mac-kin-
nons over land of no intrin-
sic value.

The shortest route to this
remote hill is via Camasunary, either by way
of the Kilmarie – Am Mam track or the coastal path
from Elgol. (Also possible by Glen Sligachan, see **walk
27**). From Camasunary, the Abhainn Camas Fhionairigh has to be waded. At low

tide one can cross near the tributary just upstream of the collapsed bridge. At high water, keep upstream until safe to cross. Follow the west bank of the river for 0.5 mile. Turn steeply up the main tributary stream issuing from the corrie ahead and to the left. Keep right of the cliffs until they recede and allow access to the broad north ridge of Sgurr na Stri. This leads to rough upper slopes comprised of a complex of rocky knolls. Keep on southward to the summit. The most southerly knoll is a glorious viewpoint above Camasunary. The knoll slightly to the north lies above great slabby cliffs plunging to Loch Coruisk, one of the most stunning glacial bowls in Britain, enclosed by the daunting serrated barrier of the wild Cuillin. Return by your outward route.

Distance from Kilmarie: 11 miles, 830m / 2723ft of ascent, 7 hours

From Elgol: 13 miles, 800m / 2625ft, 8 hours

Stalking season: walks B & D, contact Strathaird Estate tel 01471 866260

16 COIRE LAGAN AND SGURR ALASDAIR 3259ft / 993m

This short climb on clear paths into the heart of the Skye Cuillin, leads to Coire Lagan, one of the most striking rock amphitheatres in Britain, from where an optional climb is possible to the highest point on the island.

Parking is available close to Glen Brittle campsite. A stile beyond the campsite toilet block gives access to an eroded path which ascends steadily over rather wet moorland where cotton grass and bog asphodel flourish. In half a mile bear left at a path junction. As height is gained, the landscape becomes rockier. The final approach to the corrie follows the Allt Coire Lagan, passing enormous long, smooth boulders resembling beached whales. Many of the volcanic rocks appear to be covered in deep scratches or striations, the result of gouging by debris carried by a glacier.

On a fine day, the corrie is a wonderful suntrap, best seen in late afternoon. The shallow water of a lochan nestles beneath a scene of dramatic desolation. Vast slopes of talus caused by centuries of weathering, fan out into the bottom of the bowl. Above, tower the grim castellated and serrated summits of the central Cuillin; awesome, forbidding and seemingly impregnable. Tiny specks of colour are provided by the alpine lady's mantle, juniper, roseroot and rare rock whitlow grass which manage to thrive inspite of the harsh conditions. On the right stands the amazing rock pinnacle of The Chioch, a favourite climbers' playground. The seaward vista stands out in stark contrast to this wild mountain grandeur, with the long arm of Loch Brittle fronting Rum and Canna.

Non scramblers can climb Sgurr Alasdair (skoor alerstayr) 'Alexander's Peak' directly from the corrie by way of the long and tedious 'Stone Shoot'. At 1500 feet it is the longest scree run in Britain. From the head of the shoot, there is 100 feet of easy clambering to the summit. The tortuous ascent is rewarded on a clear day by extensive and superlative panoramas encompassing much of Skye and the Inner Hebrides and countless mainland peaks across an azure sea.

To vary the descent from Coire Lagan, retrace your steps for about half a mile then fork right at a path junction marked by two cairns. This descends rather boggy ground to reach the north shore of Loch an Fhir-bhallaich with fine seaward views throughout. In a further 0.75 mile, the south bank of the Banadich Burn is joined at the Eas Mor, the finest waterfall in Skye. This plunges almost 80 feet into a dramatic rocky, tree lined gorge 250 feet deep, with the Cuillins forming a spectacular backcloth. The path continues down to the road close to the stream, crossing it at a ford. If the water level is high, an easier way to the road entails following to the left, the first wall encountered at the top of the fields above Glenbrittle House. At a gap between fences, aim downhill to a Mountain Rescue Post. The road is then followed left back to the car park.

FACT FILE

Distance Coire Lagan: 5.5 miles, Height gain: 1838ft / 560m Time: 4 hours (with Sgurr Alasdair 7 miles, 3259ft/993m, 6 – 7 hours)
Start Finish: Glen Brittle campsite GR 414204 OS Sheet 32

EASIER OPTIONS

The short climb to the aforementioned Eas Mor waterfall is highly recommended, especially just after rain or if the mountains are clear behind. *(1.5 miles, 394ft/ 120m)*

Nearby, the Allt a' Choire Ghreadaidh (pronounced greeta) also boasts an impressive gorge with ferns and rowans clinging tenaciously above a beautiful series of falls. About 1.25 miles north of the road end in Glen Brittle, a path starts behind the Youth Hostel and follows the south bank of the stream. The best of the falls can be seen within 0.75 mile of the road requiring no more than 400 feet of climbing.

17 GLEN EYNORT & GLEN BRITTLE CIRCULAR

This route offers sheltered forest walking on good tracks throughout, perfect for days when gales dictate avoiding the mountain tops. Long breaks in the tree cover allow for excellent views of the dramatic rock grandeur of the Cuillin ridge above Glen Brittle which contrasts sharply to the more rounded Glen Eynort. There is an optional short climb onto An Cruachan, a superb viewpoint. The walk is particularly attractive after heavy rain, passing several fine waterfalls. Also in spring when the banks of the burns and beside the track are liberally littered with primroses, violets, bluebells, anemones and water spurge.

Three miles down Glen Eynort, fork left along the lane just before the phone box at Eynort and park near the bridge. Continue along the forest road over a cattle

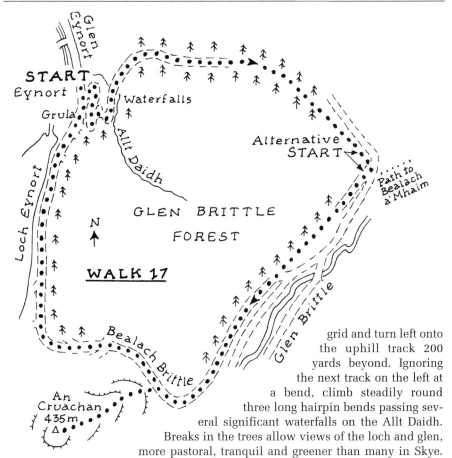

grid and turn left onto the uphill track 200 yards beyond. Ignoring the next track on the left at a bend, climb steadily round three long hairpin bends passing several significant waterfalls on the Allt Daidh. Breaks in the trees allow views of the loch and glen, more pastoral, tranquil and greener than many in Skye. Though difficult to spot, there is plenty of avian interest. I was lucky enough to spy a sea eagle a mere 100 feet above, a sparrowhawk, kestrel, robins, redstart and the tiny goldcrest.

At the next track junction, some 300 yards beyond the third hairpin, turn left. Climbing more gently, the route begins to swing round towards Glen Brittle with occasional views to the twin paps of Cnoc Scarall and later to the northern Cuillin. A tiny quarry lies on the left, a short way over the head of the climb. A few yards beyond, turn right onto a newer and stonier track. *(For the remainder of the walk keep straight on at all junctions).* This descends gently for several miles, almost meeting the Glen Brittle road opposite a picnic place GR424263 and a car park across the road from the path to the Bealach a' Mhaim GR424258 (alternative start points for the walk). Throughout this section there are vistas to the awesome Cuillin and later, along the meandering River Brittle to the loch with Rum and Canna floating serenely beyond. Views are lost for a mile as the track begins to climb gently through dense forest but large clearances approaching the Bealach

Brittle afford the finest panoramas of the day, weather permitting. Sgurr Alasdair and Sgurr Sgumain atop the hidden Coire Lagan and join the previously seen central Cuillin, given scale by the isolated youth hostel. The Eas Mor gorge on the Banadich Burn above Glen Brittle House forms a distinct gash below the moorland fronting the mountains (see **walk 16**).

From the pass, the gentle NE moorland ridge of An Cruachan (435m/ 1428ft) can be easily ascended to gain the flat elongated summit; an even finer viewpoint for the high peaks and corries of the Cuillin. With the hill being mercifully free of trees, panoramas also extend out across Loch Eynort to a multitude of lesser hills, westward to the Outer Hebrides and south to the Small Isles. The northern flanks are extremely precipitous so it is wise to retrace one's steps to the pass.

The track continues easily downhill towards Loch Eynort. Occasional breaks in the trees allow views to the Outer Hebrides beyond the cliff-girt mouth of the loch. At the head of the shallow bay, salt marsh is home to huge clumps of yellow flag iris. The gentle slopes above lead in a further 2 miles to a sizeable waterfall near the houses at Grula, close to the finish.

FACT FILE
Distance: 10.5 miles Height gain: 1200ft/ 366m Time: 5 – 5.5 hours
(with An Cruachan, 12.5 miles, 1926ft/587m, 6 – 6.5 hours)
Start/Finish: Glen Eynort GR 385271 or Glen Brittle GR 424263 or GR 424258

18 TALISKER BAY & THE MINGINISH COASTAL CIRCULAR

The main walk traverses the rough, generally pathless cliff-tops from beautiful Talisker Bay to Fiskavaig, on the striking west coast of Skye, returning inland along an easy track. Wonderful seascapes accompany you throughout the spectacular coastal section of this walk.

From the public road end at Talisker, 4 miles west of Carbost, bear right through a farmyard. (If no parking available, lay-by 0.5 mile back). The Fiskavaig track lies just beyond. It crosses a wide stream and heads to the left of A' Chailleach Farmhouse. Above, the Huisgill Burn crashes dramatically for 150 feet into a gorge. The return route allows a closer inspection later.

Abandon the track at the first sharp bend. Making use of the sheep tracks, head westwards onto the top of the 400 foot cliffs above the headland of Rubha a Cruinn. En route, a stream is crossed which leaps over the cliffs into Talisker Bay. The first of many narrow, cliff-top waterfalls along this stretch of coast. From the excellent viewpoint over the headland, turn north, away from Talisker Bay, following the straightforward cliff-tops. In about 1.5 miles, a deeply incised gorge forces a brief diversion inland. Return to the cliff edge for a further 400 yards. Beyond Rubha nan Clach, the route turns east then NE, above the wide, sheltered and entrancing Loch Bracadale. One is now forced to keep well inland of the cliff edges owing to a succession of stream cut gullies and gorges. In high winds, the spray from the waterfalls plunging over the cliffs, can be flung back inland for several hundred yards.

Continue above the coast onto the hill overlooking the headland of Gob na h-Oa, a fine viewpoint for the striking cliff-girt coast you have just traversed. The remains of an Iron Age broch above and to the right, commands a fine strategic position. From the headland turn south to join the Fiskavaig road. At a hairpin bend, carry on southward onto the track leading across the open heather moorland to the Huisgill Burn. Seabirds give way to stonechats, whinchats, buzzards, wheatears and pipits. As the path zigzags back down to Talisker, you pass close to the Eas Mor waterfall and can enjoy charming views of the waterfalls in Talisker Bay. *Distance 8 miles, approx 1000ft/ 304m of ascent, 5 – 5.5 hours* *Start/ Finish: road end Talisker GR 326306 OS Sheet 32*

WALK 18

EASY OPTIONS

Talisker Bay is an entrancing location on a fine day and is reached by an easy stroll. From the public road end, keep left along the private road past Talisker House. It is set in an idyllic situation, with its own private grounds, surrounded by sheltering trees and blazing yellow gorse, dominated by the precipitous cliffs of Preshal More; a small peak which appears to have no easy side. A Land-Rover track beyond the house, passes flowery banks and in 0.75 mile reaches the black sandy beach. On the south side of the bay, a line of impressive cliffs ends with the overhanging sea stack of Stac an Fhucadair at Talisker Point. *At LOW TIDE* it is possible to boulder hop along a wave cut platform and reach the stack. A waterfall plunges straight down the more broken cliffs above the northern shore whilst to seaward lies South Uist. Gulls, shags, kittiwakes and fulmars are likely to provide the avian interest. Return by your outward route. *2.5 miles, allow 1.5 hours*

Also worthwhile and not unduly difficult (being on good tracks and paths) is to follow the last section of the main walk from Talisker to the viewpoint hill overlooking the Gob na h-Oa headland near Fiskavaig. Again return by the outward route. *6 miles, 656ft/ 200 metres of ascent, 3 – 3.5 hours*

For those interested in whisky, any of the above can be combined with a guided tour of Talisker Distillery, some 4 miles to the east, at Carbost on Loch Harport. *Open Monday – Friday, April – October.* Also at Carbost is a folk museum, *open daily 10am – 6pm.*

19 ORBOST TO MACLEOD'S MAIDENS

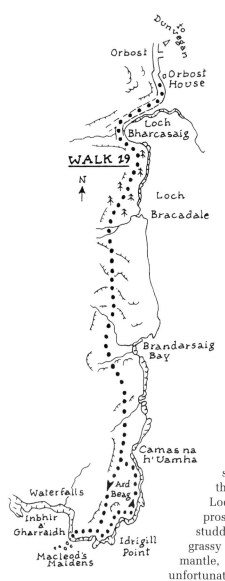

This coastal walk is justifiably well known and popular. However, what is not so well known is that walkers who religiously follow the distinct path there and back, miss out on much of the superb scenery. This will be especially true in years to come as much of the first 3 miles are being planted with trees. Views are already limited near the start but considerable rewards come later, so persevere! Except during a prolonged drought, the route should be avoided if you don't like bog or boulder hopping numerous streams. Boots are essential and gaiters and a stick recommended.

Park by the farm at the road end near Orbost House, 4 miles south of Dunvegan, ensuring farm access is not blocked. The rough continuation of the road down to the houses at Barcasaig Bay used to be easy to drive but is now hideous and liable to damage low slung cars. Far better to walk. Beyond the buildings, the track crosses a bridge and ascends gently through dense forest for about a mile. Beyond a burn, a usually boggy path climbs the moorland upto a small pass. Whilst the trees are still young, there are occasionally good views out across Loch Bracadale. Accompanied by a fine prospect to Rum and across the cliff-girt, island studded bay, the route now descends into a wide grassy river valley carpeted with violets, lady's mantle, celandines, thyme, St John's Wort and unfortunately, new coniferous plantings. Beyond some ruined crofts, a pretty stream is crossed just above a gorge lined with rowans and studded in primroses. Small waterfalls abound along the entire course of the river.

The worst of the bog is now behind you. From the head of the next rise, there are extensive views along the west coast of Skye towards the Cuillins. The line of high cliffs running from Rubha nan Clach to Fiskavaig Bay are particularly striking with numerous hanging waterfalls tumbling straight into the sea. On a windy day, one can clearly see the distant spray being blown several hundred yards backwards over the cliff tops. The path descends to a gate by a stream. Take note as this is where you will rejoin the path on the homeward leg. Continue through a small pass where sheep tracks may cause some confusion. The path keeps to the right side of the defile, a little way above the marshy floor, then swings SW across moorland to reach a cairn on an airy crumbling cliff top directly above the three sea stacks known as MacLeod's Maidens. The respective dumpy and thin Daughters are chaperoned by the Mother 207 feet high, first climbed in 1959. To the west stand the superb cliffs of Inbhir a' Gharraidh with two hanging waterfalls. On a clear day, panoramas extend to the Small Isles and the Outer Hebrides.

Leave the path and head eastward along the easy grassy cliff tops taking time to venture out onto some of the promontories for more breathtaking seascapes and views of the nesting shags and kittiwakes. Turning north beyond Idrigill Point, use a wide grassy corridor between wee crags to ascend the small hill of Ard Beag which projects tall cliffs towards Loch Bracadale and is inhabited by black rabbits and a mass of violets. Keep to the seaward side just below the summit, making use of the sheep tracks. As you begin to descend northward from the hill, an unusual double natural arch and several caves come into view across the bay of Camas na h-Uamha backed by a succession of cliffs and afforested hills. Continue easily along the cliff top above the arches before swinging across the grass to rejoin the path and your outward route.

FACT FILE
Distance: 10.5 miles, Height gain: 450m/ 1477ft
Time: 5 – 7 hours
Start/ Finish: Orbost GR 257432 OS Sheet 23

EASY OPTION
The start of the main walk from Orbost House to pretty Loch Barcasaig is dry underfoot and provides an easy and scenic stroll of 1.25 miles return. Seals can often be seen close to shore plus a variety of birds.

20 NEIST POINT (SKYE)

This short outing explores the cliff-girt headland of Neist Point which projects into striking Moonen Bay, dominated by the 971 foot rock prow of Waterstein Head. Paths are clear and easy and boots are not essential.

The narrow Waterstein road west of Colbost on Loch Dunvegan, ends at a large car park 1200 yards from the lighthouse above the point. Some 100 feet of steep steps lead down to an easy path traversing the clipped grassy cliff-tops to the lighthouse which looks out across The Minch to the Outer Hebrides. An optional, entertaining scramble can be found on the huge rock pavement between the lighthouse and Neist Point itself. To appreciate the grandeur of the 300 foot cliffs, it is worth making easy detours from the path on your return. Rather than return directly to the car park, keep left above the sea. A path follows the top of 400 foot cliffs patrolled by shags, gannets and kittiwakes to reach the ruins of a coastguard look-out station. Continue for a further 500 yards across the cliff tops for the prospect across Oisgill Bay to the spectacular 645 ft cliffs of Biod Ban. Rejoin the path back to the car park.

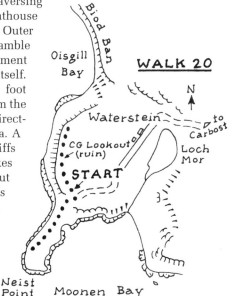

FACT FILE
Distance: 3 miles
Time: 1.5 – 2 hours
Start / Finish: Waterstein road end GR 133477

F **6lor those** wishing to explore this magnificent coastline further, return along the road for 1.5 miles to the pass above Loch Mor. Easy grassy slopes can be followed southward above the cliffs of Moonen Bay to reach the summit of Waterstein Head in 1.5 miles. To enjoy the cliffs further south, an alternative is to continue along the road for a further 1.5 miles then bear right on to the Ramasaig road. The cliff tops can be reached from numerous points en route. From Ramasaig itself, a path leads inland across the moorland to reach remote Lorgill Bay.

The above can be combined with interesting visits to the nearby: **Blackhouse Folk Museum** near Colbost (*April – Oct*), the **Glendale Toy Museum** (*open all year, Mon – Sat*) and **Dunvegan Castle** (*April – Oct*), the seat of Clan Macleod since the 13th century, although the present castle only dates from the 1840s.

21 GALTRIGILL TO 'SKY CLIFF'

This short walk crosses rough moorland to reach the highest sea cliff on Skye, a superb viewpoint. There is an optional extension to an unusual natural arch.

Take the minor road winding above the western shore of Loch Dunvegan to the road end by the ruins of old Galtrigill. It is possible to park here but ensure sufficient space is left for vehicles to turn. Walk straight on over the grazing land towards the gorge of the Galtrigill Burn then make for the obvious stile just to the right of a ruin. Go over a second stile and head upstream a short way above the flowery banks. Cross the river once above the gorge then over a gate in the fence just above. Making use of good sheep tracks, follow the fence gently uphill. This eventually turns away from the river but continue ahead just above the north bank. When the stream peters out, keep straight on over the heather moorland to gain the close cropped grassy cliff top. Follow this northward onto Biod an Athair,

'Sky Cliff', 313m/ 1027ft. The trig point stands only a yard away from an abrupt drop to the crashing waves. It is only safe to view the cliffs by lying down. To better appreciate the scale of the dramatic cliffs, continue easily northward, descending the gentle cliff top for about half a mile. On a clear day, the prospect to the Western Isles, Small Isles and across Loch Dunvegan to the distant Cuillin, are equally enthralling.

Either retrace your steps or for those who are happy crossing very rough and often marshy moorland, head eastward to the cliff top overlooking Loch Dunvegan and Am Famhair. Sea level changes and erosion have left this unique natural arch perched on dry land and free standing away from the cliff. To return, follow the cliff edge southward for about 600 yards then veer a little inland over the moorland to regain the Galtrigill Burn above its deep gorge.

Distance: 5 miles Height gain: 280m/ 919ft Time: 4 hours
Start/ Finish: Galtrigill GR 181546 OS Sheet 23

The above can be combined with a visit to the nearby **Borreraig Park Exhibition Croft** (*daily 9am – 6pm*), a huge open air museum of traditional horse drawn machinery. Also the **Glendale Toy Museum**, (*Mon – Sat*) for children of all ages!

22 THE WATERNISH PENINSULA

This quiet corner of northern Skye offers several easy routes in an area rich in historical association, seabird activity and wide seascapes extending to the Outer Hebrides.

Trumpan to Waternish Point Park in the large lay-by near the ruins of Trumpan Church above Ardmore Bay (GR 225612). The church was burnt in 1578 by the Macdonalds who raided from Uist. Only a few defenders lived to tell the tale and none of the raiders. Follow the road NW from the church for 500 yards to a right angled bend. Bear left through a gate onto a good track. Follow this gently over the heather moorland above the rocky coast, enjoying the seascapes throughout. The route passes under a memorial cairn to Roderick MacLeod of Unish who died here in battle circa 1530, fighting the Madonalds of Trotternish. You later pass a ruined croft and the remains of Dun Borrafiach Iron-Age broch. Further on, another broch, Dun Gearymore, is easier to reach though it is in a more ruinous state. A short way beyond this second broch, the track bears right to the ruins of Unish, further sad reminders of the Highland Clearances. Alternatively one can leave the track and follow the easy cliff-tops to the lighthouse at Waternish Point. It was here that Bonnie Prince Charlie, dressed as the maid Betty Burke, arrived with Flora Macdonald in 1746 after fleeing in a small boat from the Hanovarian soldiers on South Uist. Return the same way.

Easy 6 miles, allow 3 hours

Ardmore Peninsula From Trumpan Church turn left along the road and descend a short steep hill. A track on your right now leads across grazing land to the sandy shores of Ardmore Bay, a great place for viewing wading birds. Continue just above the shore to the tip of the tiny peninsula, a delightful viewpoint. From Ardmore Point, a path leads back to Trumpan following the flowery low cliff-tops northward on the west side of the peninsula. A natural arch is passed en route. From the cliffs of Ard Bead, a fine view opens out northward along the Waternish Peninsula with numerous coastal waterfalls. Shags colonise a small bay beyond, also popular with seals. Trumpan is reached in a further 500 yards.

2.5 miles, allow 1.5 hours

These walks could be combined with a visit to **Skyeskyns**, a unique and traditional sheepskin tannery. Guided tours are offered round the workshop (*daily April – Oct*).

23 THE QUEER QUIRAING

Quiraing (pronounced kooraing) is the Gaelic for 'pillared stronghold.' Popular with tourists since Victorian times, this awesome rocky landscape in north Skye, is even more bizarre that that of the Storr. The spectacular shattered pinnacles and cliffs are the result of differential weathering and huge landslips; the slow downward slide of layers of volcanic rock following the retreat of the glaciers some 10,000 years ago. This short but exciting walk ventures into the heart of the Quiraing before returning over the cliff-tops above. The awkward climb to the curious 'Table' is optional.

The main path starts from the large lay-by at the Bealach Ollasgaiste, the pass on the road between Uig and Staffin. This path at the base of the cliffs crosses several potentially awkward gullies. An alternative path begins about 700 yards down the road to the east. It ascends easily over close cropped grass towards the cliffs, to join the main path. This levels out and leads NE to The Prison, a huge, precipitous sided rock slab which resembles castle battlements. Above and to the left, towers The Needle, a 120 foot overhanging obelisk.

The easiest route passes **The Prison** then turns northward, still hugging the base of the cliffs. An optional ascent to **The Table**, later joins this path a few hundred yards further on. This steep climb is on a badly eroded and loose path, only suitable for very

sure footed walkers. A cairn marks the start of the path, which climbs to the left of **The Needle**, crosses a gully above and to the right, then passes through a maze of assorted towers and contorted pinnacles to reach The Table. Surrounded by tall cliffs, this almost flat piece of turf atops a rectangular rock tower, 120ft x 60ft wide. It was once used for hiding cattle from raiders and more recently, for a shinty match. Partial erosion of the encircling rock walls allows glimpses of the sea, moorland and lochans way below, fronting the Inner Isles and the mainland.

Return to the foot of The Table. To its right (on the north side), a cairn marks the head of a wide gully. Although steep and eroded, it is less so than the path of ascent and has plenty of reassuring solid rocks to the sides for handholds. The stones give way to terraced grass and the aforementioned path traversing beneath the cliffs and pinnacles. Continue northward along the main path, ignoring any paths forking right. The landscape becomes greener and you pass several tiny lochans and the pinnacles of **Leac nan Fionn** on your right.

Aim for the col to the north of **Meall na Suiramach**; a break in the cliffs allows access to the ridge above. A short gentle detour northward, along the edge of the cliffs, gains the summit of **Sron Vourlinn** 378m/ 1242ft and an excellent prospect seaward. Retrace your steps to the col, then follow the cliff-top, initially steeply, then quite gently, swinging southward. Enjoy the magnificent views down the plunging buttresses to The Table and its satellites and beyond to the Sound of Raasay and the Applecross mountains. Another worthwhile short detour heads westward onto the actual summit of **Meall na Suiramach** 543m / 1782ft, an even more extensive viewpoint for the mainland and Outer Hebrides. Descend the steepening grassy slopes now to the **Bealach Ollasgiarte**, keeping slightly westward, away from the cliffs, for the last 0.75 mile, to avoid difficult precipitous ground. Sheep tracks can aid progress. *Take great care on this final section should mist descend.*

FACT FILE
Distance: 5.5 miles, 1445ft/ 440m of ascent
Time 4 – 4.5 hours
Start / Finish: Uig – Staffin road at either Bealach Ollasgairte GR 440679 or GR 444682 OS Sheet 23
Remarks: In poor weather, only the lower section of the walk is recommended
Public Transport: Occasional buses from Portree pass through Staffin, 1.5 miles from start

24 BEINN EDRA CIRCULAR

The complex Trotternish Ridge dominates the north of Skye. Reaching a high point of only 2360 feet, this majestic range of hills is often clear when the Cuillins further south are completely shrouded in cloud for days. Easy grassy slopes to the west lead gently to a dramatic escarpment plunging abruptly in the east to desolate boggy moorland and a scattering of white houses dotted along the fertile coastal fringes. The cliffs and strange pinnacles of The Storr and Quiraing are the most celebrated points along the ridge. This short circular hillwalk leaves the crowds behind and ventures onto Beinn Edra, 2006ft / 611m, a superb viewpoint sandwiched between its more illustrious neighbours.

From Uig, take the single track road climbing into Glen Conan. One can usually park near the road end outside the last croft but ensure farm access is not blocked. Follow the track which swings easily uphill above the River Conan. At the head of the glen, an arc of three waterfalls plunge attractively through small but deeply incised gorges. Across the wide valley, near the road end in Glen Uig, lie a clutch of unusual large rocky dimples, formed by volcanic cone sheets. The route emerges onto open heather moorland. Moorland birds are prolific and include

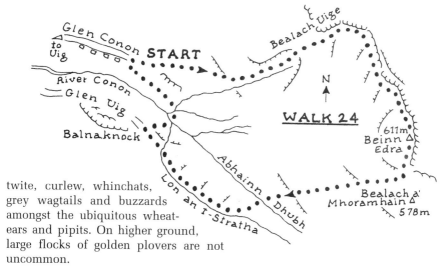

twite, curlew, whinchats, grey wagtails and buzzards amongst the ubiquitous wheatears and pipits. On higher ground, large flocks of golden plovers are not uncommon.

After about a mile, the track disappears by some peat cuttings. Skirt above these, cross the fence ahead and follow it a short distance down to the stream on the right. An indistinct, often wet path now follows above the stream, which in its upper reaches tumbles in a series of small waterfalls. The path continues onto the spine of the Trotternish ridge, meeting it just south of the Bealach Uige, about 1.25 miles NNW of the summit of Beinn Edra. Should you lose the path in the bog en route, simply continue over the rough ground towards the ridge. After 2 miles of rounded, undistinguished slopes, the vistas from the cliff rim are as sensational as they are sudden and accompany you all the way to the domed summit. The series of sheer cliffs, pinnacles, buttresses and gullies of Trotternish hold the attention as much as the panoramas which extend to the Outer Hebrides, Uig Bay, Torridon, Applecross, Assynt and the far north. On reaching the trig point, the distant Cuillin hove into view, fronted by the tall cliffs of The Storr.

Continue south down the edge of the scarp to the next col, the Bealach a' Mhoramhain. A path close to a grassy dyke descends easily to the lowest of the pretty waterfalls on the Abhainn Dhubh. Cross the river (if in spate, it is easier 400 yards upstream) then follow the path SW to reach the good track on the north bank of the racing stream, the Lon an t-Sratha. Before this track, the path can get rather lost in the bog, so you may need to keep to the drier heathery hummocks and aim for the river. After a mile, the track crosses the stream on easy stepping stones (unless in spate) and leads down to Balnaknock. It is usually possible to work a way around the head of the glen, crossing the River Conan and the grazing flats to reach your starting point. In spate conditions you may need to continue downstream to the bridge below number 9 croft in Glen Conan, then follow the road back.

FACT FILE
Distance: 7.5 miles Height gain: 1772ft / 540m
Time: 4 – 5 hours
Start / Finish: head of Glen Conan GR 418637 OS Sheet 23
Remarks: some river crossings awkward immediately after heavy rain.
Stalking season: contact Scottish office Agricultural Dept. Estates Office Tel 01478
612516
Public Transport: buses from Portree to Uig pass within 1.7 miles of the start

EASY OPTIONS
The quiet road climbing into Glen Uig from Uig Bay provides easy and pleasant walking with good views over the harbour. It passes through a delightful wooded section and in the upper valley, the volcanic cone sheet field. The waterfalls are also well displayed near Balnaknock. Uig harbour itself is also worthy of a stroll. There is a path along the southern shore of the bay beginning near the bridge on the south bank of the River Conan.

The above can be combined with a visit to the **Skye Museum of Island Life** at Kilmuir, 5 miles north of Uig. A group of seven thatched cottages show life on the island 100 years ago (*open April – Oct.*) Two miles further north, lie the ruins of **Duntulm Castle** in a very picturesque setting.

25 THE STORR AND THE OLD MAN

This short hillwalk climbs into one of the most amazing rock landscapes in Britain, cradled beneath The Storr 719m/ 2359ft. For the average walker, the corrie bowl known as The Sanctuary, makes a superb destination with spectacular deeply fissured rock buttresses towering over a curious collection of shattered pinnacles and castellated tops, riven over the centuries by frost, wind and rain. The bowl displays classic landslip topography, following the collapse of sedimentary layers of rock under the weight of intruding volcanic lava. The highest pinnacle, known as The Old Man, is one of Skye's most famous landmarks, well seen when driving north from Portree approaching Loch Fada. In clear weather hillwalkers may wish to extend the walk by ascending The Storr itself, a superb viewpoint and the highest point on the long Trotternish Escarpment.

The main path to the Sanctuary begins at the large Forestry Commission car park under The Storr, just north of Loch Leathan. Inspite of recent improvements, expect to encounter some wet and boggy patches after rain. Except during a drought, it is preferable to continue north along the road for a short distance to the edge of the trees. A path ascends near the fence on the north side of the forest. Entrancing views open out over Loch Leathan and Loch Fada to the Cuillins, Raasay and the mainland mountains. The five huge serrated buttresses of The Storr reminded me of the Italian Dolomites on a miniature scale. Although only 650 feet high, they appear taller.

Beyond the top forest fence, the pinnacles are reached over a short steep stretch of moorland. According to local legend, the Old Man and his Wife (who now lies horizontally) were carried here on a wave. They reputedly saw something that no human should ever see and were turned to stone as a result. The Old Man is a leaning, pear-shaped obelisk, 160 feet tall with an undercut base. Inspite of its crumbly texture, it has been climbed. There are a dozen pinnacles altogether to explore, one of which, The Needle, has three keyhole arches or eyes. Crevices in the cliffs and pinnacles are home to a profusion of flora including mossy and purple saxifrage, roseroot, moss campion, mountain sorrel, northern rock-cress and the rare, tiny green petalled Icelandic Purslane. Retrace your steps unless climbing The Storr.

To ascend The Storr, head northward from the pinnacles, climbing gently beneath the sheer cliffs until they dramatically reduce in height and are eventually left behind. The path disappears too but easy if somewhat eroded scree, soil and grass leads up onto the ridge. Small rocky outcrops allow for occasional, optional easy scrambling. Those with a good head for heights should ascend the ridge near the rim of the eastern cliffs. With care it is possible to peer down many of the great clefts, their sheer broken walls often framing the Old Man and his Guardians hundreds of feet below. The pinnacles suddenly seem insignificant. There are breathtaking views throughout the climb to the mainland over the Sound of Raasay. The Skye delights on show include the Quiraing, Leac nan Fionn, the Cuillins and the impressive escarpment of the Trotternish hills. Approaching the summit, a short tract of path emerges. From the trig point, the striking 360 degree panoramas extend to the Outer Hebrides and Sutherland.

In descent, take a similar line to the ascent but keep away from the cliff edges. Make use of the grassy terraces to avoid most of the eroded slopes. Rejoin the path leading back to the pinnacles. A scenically attractive alternative descent follows the edge of the escarpment cliffs steeply southward to the Bealach Beag, then more gently over two minor rises to the Bealach Mor. From here, a break in the cliffs allows a short steep descent eastward to the gradual moorland slopes above Loch Leathan. The road is gained about 1.5 miles south of the start point.

67

FACT FILE

Distance: Storr walk 5 miles , 1800ft/ 550m of ascent, 4 – 5 hours
To the Sanctuary return: 2.5 miles, 885ft/ 270m 2.5 hours
Start/ Finish: 6.5 miles north of Portree on A855 GR 511531 OS Sheet 23
Remarks: Boots essential, gaiters recommended after rain
Public Transport: occasional buses from Portree encircle the Trotternish Peninsula,
passing the start

26 ASCENT OF BRUACH NA FRITHE 3143ft/935m

The Cuillin ridge of Skye is a 7 mile long twisting, serrated edge, topped by sharp peaks, liberally laced with dizzy pinnacles, plunging ridges, buttresses and gullies; stark, sensational and unforgettable. Its name derives from the Norse, Kjollen, 'keel shaped ridges'. Only one summit can be attained without exposed scrambling and with hands in pockets; Bruach na Frithe, (broo-ach na free-ha), *'slope of the forest'*. An added attraction for non scrambling walkers is that it is probably the finest viewpoint along the entire ridge, worth saving for a fine day.

A private road leaves the A863 road about 0.5 mile west of Sligachan Hotel and heads past Alldearg House. A path continues SW towards the Bealach a' Mhaim above the left bank of the Allt Dearg Mor; an entertaining and highly photogenic river in spate. (For those staying in Glen

Brittle, an alternative path leading to the pass, leaves the road at the edge of a large forest plantation some 4.5 miles south of the junction with the B8009). Both paths cross peaty moorland which is inclined to be wet except during a long drought. From the pass, a path ascends the steep scree and grass of the NW ridge of Bruach na Frithe, a haven for ptarmigan. If you disturb a hen ptarmigan in May, June or July, you may well see her feigning injury; running away from her nest or chicks dragging a wing along the ground, to distract intruders from her eggs or well camouflaged young. The ridge becomes increasingly rocky and narrows considerably over the last 800 feet with optional scrambling opportunities along the crest, away from the path.

Seen close to, the surrounding peaks and corries appear almost frightening, wild and impregnable. The three great twists in the main Cuillin ridge, create a very striking picture. Differential weathering and erosion of the gabbro and basalt intrusions, have created awesome contortions in the rock. The views to the rest of the island and to seaward are equally breathtaking. From the summit, follow the gentle path eastward down to the Bealach nan Lice, then head out along the south ridge of Sgurr a' Bhasteir for a superb view of Sgurr na Gillean's Pinnacle Ridge and the Bhasteir Tooth. From Bruach na Frithe, this dramatic prow of rock goes unnoticed, its rocks merging in with those of Am Bhasteir. From certain angles however, the Tooth resembles one of the huge stone men of Easter Island or the cowled head of a priest.

To complete a spectacular circular round, return to the main ridge and descend NE under Am Bhasteir into scree riddled Coire a' Bhasteir. A cairned path is eventually joined above and to the west of the Allt Dearg Beag which has gouged a considerable gorge. The path follows this lively river for about a mile, before cutting across the moorland back to Sligachan.

FACT FILE

Distance: 8 miles, with height gain 3084ft / 940m
Time: 6 hours
Start/ Finish: Sligachan GR 485298 OS 1:50,000 Sheet 32 or OS 1:25,000 Cuillins/ Torridon sheet
Remarks: Owing to the featureless lower ground, the walk is not recommended to the inexperienced in low hillfog. Difficult under winter conditions.
Stalking: contact MacLeod Estate tel. 01478 640335 or 640404
Public Transport: Kyle to Broadford & Portree buses pass start

EASY OPTION

The first part of the main walk along the Allt Dearg Mor makes for an attractive short outing, especially when the river level is high.

27 LOCH CORUISK & SGURR NA STRI FROM SLIGACHAN (SKYE)

Loch Coruisk is one of the remotest scenic gems in Skye; a striking glacial bowl encircled by the awesome, serrated rocky barrier of the Cuillin mountains. The peaks are set back from the island studded, sandy fringed loch, so they tend to inspire rather than intimidate. Although approachable from Elgol, potentially awkward river crossings and an occasionally tricky coastal path may deter many. The approach via Glen Sligachan is the easiest, though longer route. Similarly with the peak of Sgurr na Stri overlooking the loch; arguably the finest viewpoint on the island (see also **walk 15D**). The glen cuts a dramatic swathe between the rounded scree domes of the Red Cuillin and the contrasting higher and more jagged towers and pinnacles of the Black Cuillin, with their wild and complex corries.

From the old bridge near the Sligachan Inn, take the obvious though sometimes wet path southward along Glen Sligachan. At the foot of Am Fraoch-choire, some 4 miles along the glen, keep right at the path junction on the right side of a burn. A rising traverse on a drier and rockier path gains a cairn on Druim Hain. Keep left to reach a second cairn. Here you have the choice of either forking right and descending in a thousand feet to Loch Coruisk via Loch a' Choire Riabhaich or bearing left and continuing upward onto Sgurr na Stri. The latter path traverses below Sgurr Hain to pass just above a memorial cairn to Captain Maryon who died here in 1946. A short way on, a shallow grassy bowl allows an easy ascent to the complicated rocky knolls forming the summit area. Keep southward to the summit, the most southerly knoll; an arresting viewpoint above Camasunary. The knoll slightly to the north looks out along the full length of Loch Coruisk. For those wishing to explore the loch more closely, large slabby cliffs prevent a direct descent but it is possible to descend to Loch a' Choire Riabhaich and then join the path down.

Paths run along both sides of the loch and those with the time and energy could encircle the loch. Bear in mind however that it is long way back and the stepping stones across the River Scavaig at the mouth of the loch, can be difficult if not impossible after heavy rain.

FACT FILE

Distance Loch Coruisk return 15 miles, 660m / 2165ft of ascent, 8 hours
Distance Sgurr na Stri return 15 miles, 620m / 2034ft of ascent, 8 hours (if descending to Loch Coruisk, 16 miles, 930m / 3050ft, 9.5 hours)
Start/ Finish: Sligachan Inn GR 487299
Stalking: Strathaird Estate tel. 01471 866260
Public Transport: Kyle – Portree buses pass start

EASIER OPTIONS

Take a boat trip! Trips are available to Loch Coruisk from Elgol; the 'Bella Jane' tel. enquiries 01471 866244, bookings 0800 733089 *April – Oct* or the 'Nicola' tel 01471 866236 *May – Oct.* They usually allow *1 – 2 hours* ashore.

The aforementioned path along Glen Sligachan is worthy of exploration for however far is desired. Being a secluded glen, there is plenty of avian and floral interest in addition to the drama of the mountainous backcloth. After heavy rain it is worth detouring off the path and following the attractive Allt Dairich which has cut a tree-lined ravine. There are impressive falls at GR 492294 about 500 yards from the Sligachan Inn. This could be combined with a visit to the **Luib Folk Museum** on nearby Loch Ainort (*April – Oct*) or **The Serpentarium** at Broadford (*Easter – Oct*).

Glen Sligachan

N.B. North is not at the top of this map

Am Fraoch -choire

WALK 27

Druim Hain

Loch a' Choire Riabhaich

Sgurr Hain

Walk 15D to Camasunary

optional descent

Loch Coruisk

Sgurr na Stri 497m

Loch Scavaig

28 RIVER LAIR & THE COULIN PASS

This circular walk explores the dramatic valleys north of Achnashellach in Glen Carron. The combination of boisterous rivers, mixed woodland and shapely rocky peaks, will impress at any time but particularly after heavy rain. There are good paths throughout and all potentially difficult river crossings are bridged. The first part of the walk is worth doing even on a poor day, given the numerous waterfalls and attractive forest.

From the A890 at Achnashellach, follow the lane to the railway station. Turn left at the station and take the track for about 100 yards. Cross the railway line and go through a gate. A generally good path rises steadily through the forest above the east bank of the River Lair. The whole area is one beautiful mass of pines,

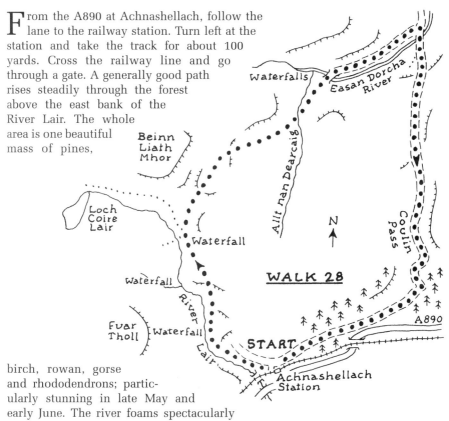

birch, rowan, gorse and rhododendrons; particularly stunning in late May and early June. The river foams spectacularly through a narrow rocky wood lined gorge, dropping 1100 feet over 1.25 miles in a series of falls, rapids and water chutes. There are three main sets of falls. Side-tracks lead to the lower falls. The middle series are seen several hundred yards away. The upper falls lie beside the track. The path emerges onto open moorland below majestic cliff-girt Fuar Tholl and the wild ridges of Beinn Liath Mhor and Sgorr Ruadh with their flanking acres of scree and broken crags.

At a path junction just above the upper falls, keep right. Bear right again at a second junction nearby. (If time and energy permits, it is worthwhile turning left at this second junction and making a detour to Loch Coire Lair, a mile beyond. It lies in an impressive bowl surrounded by the Coulin Forest peaks. The great Mainreachan buttress of Fuar Tholl hoves into view, a climbers' playground). The main path crosses a watershed and descends gently to the Easan Dorcha river. This is joined by the Allt nan Dearcaig just below a significant waterfall. Together they cascade some 300 feet to a footbridge at the foot of the Coulin Pass. Follow the path down to the bridge. Cross the river to join the track climbing gently southward to the Coulin Pass. Ignore the path bearing right at the head of the pass and keep on the main track into the forest. Keep left at a major track junction in a further 1.25 miles. Achnashellach Station is reached in a further 0.5 mile.

FACT FILE
Distance:9 miles 1560ft/476m of ascent 5 – 6 hours
Start / Finish: Achnashellach Station GR 003484 OS Sheet 25
Public Transport: Inverness – Kyle trains stop at Achnashellach

29 ASCENT OF BIDEAN A' CHOIRE SHEASGAICH 3102 ft / 945m & LURG MHOR 3234 ft / 986m

Lovers of solitude and wilderness will relish this strenuous traverse of two of the remotest Munros. Bidean a' Choire Sheasgaich (beedyan a kora hesgeech) *'peak of the corrie of the fallow cattle',* must rank as one of the finest hills in Scotland being dramatic in shape, challenging and exhilarating in its ascent and with a summit view par excellence. The area is also a rich habitat for flora and fauna including eagles, snow bunting and innumerable deer.

From Craig in Glen Carron, cross the railway line and take the forest track climbing steeply eastward through Achnashellach Forest. If the gate is unlocked, there seems to be no objection to cars being driven up to the top edge of the forest, which reduces the day's exertions considerably. If locked, a cycle is invaluable, more so for the freewheel back later in the day. Just check your brakes first!

Beyond the tree-line, a dramatic view of the Coulin Forest mountains opens up to the north. The track continues more gently beneath the craggy western flanks of Sgurr nan Ceannaichean, close to the Allt a' Chonais, the habitat of grey herons and dippers. About 1.5 miles beyond the forest, a bridge crosses the river (any cycles will have to be left here) and a clearly defined, though somewhat boggy, path leads gently up to the Bealach Bhearnais. The Corbett, Beinn Tarsuinn, lies between you and the first Munro. Be warned, it is easier to climb over this rough hill than attempt to skirt round it. A steep climb over grass and boulders gains the first top on the long but easy summit ridge. Bidean a' Choire Sheasgaich is seen at its best, appearing as a shapely imposing peak with its intimidating north ridge rising abruptly in tiers of crags. Vistas extend to the Torridons, Shiel hills and across the shimmering sea to Skye, Rum and Eigg. Eastward, Loch Monar fills the view, a kaleidoscope of blues and reflections, nestling amongst wild Munros.

From the summit, descend SW to a small lochan on the ridge. Apart from one short scramble, the going is grassy as you follow the ridge to the col between the summit and west top. A steep, diagonal descent brings the low narrow col of Bealach an Sgoltaidh 550m. Large crags now confront you but a steep grassy line wends through the first difficulties. The ridge could be a confusing nightmare in thick fog. In clear weather however, route selection is easy; there being little in the way of alternatives. I faced only one short awkward scramble. Above the initial broken ring of crags, lies a rock band strung right across the ridge. The one breach in its defences is a path cutting up a narrow grassy gully. Above, the going flattens out for a time and narrow grassy corridors lead through a succession of small rock bands. A small lochan, deep enough for a swim, would be very tempting on a hot day. The final steep climb up a narrowing ridge, wends in and out of yet more crags. There is certainly nothing easy about Bidean a' Choire Sheasgaich! From the cairn, I lost count of the mountains on view. My eyes were also drawn to the Hebrides across the dazzling Inner Sound.

A steep descent brings a much broader and straightforward ridge leading directly to the summit of Lurg Mhor *'long shank'* (looroog voar). Moss and thrift carpet the grassy sections although the terrain is often quite steep and rocky.

Having retraced your steps to the col under Bidean a' Choire Sheasgaich, make a gently rising traverse beneath the WSW ridge, joining the crest after some 600 yards. *Do not* leave the ridge before the col just NE of the knoll, Sail Riabhach, or you may become snarled up in crags. From the col, turn due north and descend steeply into Strath Bearneas. Coire Seasgach is riddled with crags upto 50 feet high and may necessitate the occasional small

Craig A890
START
Achnashellach
Forest
Sgurr nan Ceannaich
Allt a' Chonais
N
WALK 29
Bealach Bhearnais
Strath Bearneas
Beinn Tharsuinn
△863m
Bealach an Sgoltaidh
Coire Seasgach
Sail Riabhach
△945m
△Bidean a'Choire Sheasgaich
Lurg Mhor
△986m

diversion. In early summer, an abundance of violets, butterwort and orchids add bright splashes of colour to an already impressive scene. In this idyllic glen, I was lucky enough to spot lizards, an army of bouncing frogs and an eagle.

Once over some peaty hummocks littering the lower slopes of Beinn Tarsuinn, traces of a path lead gently back up to the Bealach Bhearnais, wending through grassy and peaty moraines. Your outward route is then followed back to Craig.

For Munro baggers who like backpacking, the above can be included as part of a splendid two day expedition from Craig. On day one follow the Allt a' Chonais as per above for a further 2 miles then climb Sgurr a' Charoachain by its long but easy grassy NE ridge. Continue along the narrow ridge to Sgurr Choinnich then descend west to the Bealach Bhearnais, a fine wild camping site. On day two follow the aforementioned route over Bidean a' Choire Sheasgaich etc.

FACT FILE
Distance from Craig: 18.5 miles Height gain: 4760ft/1450m
Start/ Finish: Craig in Glen Carron GR 040493 OS Sheet 25
Remarks: Not recommended to the inexperienced in adverse weather or under snow.
Public transport: Kyle of Lochalsh-Inverness railway stops at Achnashellach.
Stalking season: contact Attadale Estate Stalker Tel. 01520 722308

EASY OPTION
Providing you can drive up through the forest from Craig, the path beside the Allt a' Chonais makes for a quiet, gentle and pleasurable outing.
See also **Walk 28** from Achnashellach

30 LOCHCARRON NATURE RESERVE

The Allt nan Carnan, 'the burn of the cairns', flows into Loch Carron beyond a deep, narrow gorge on the western fringes of Lochcarron village. In its upper reaches, the river has an even larger gorge, 1200 yards long and upto 80 feet deep with a fine waterfall at its head (GR 897412). The gorges and slopes just above are heavily wooded and have been designated as a nature reserve. Oak and birch predominate but hazel, aspen ash, rowan, wild rose, bird cherry and wych elm also thrive along with a profusion of ferns, mosses and woodland flowers.

To access the reserve, start at the road bridge at the western end of Lochcarron, opposite the road junction to Strome. *Sure-footed walkers only* can venture about 300 yards along the

impressive lower gorge to a large waterfall. Go through the gate on the west bank then immediately cross to the east bank (the apparent path along the left bank fizzles-out very quickly). The path is very narrow and often sloping with fallen trees to step over. When it peters out, carefully follow the greasy, mossy boulders at the side of the river until the waterfall hoves into view. Return the same way.

The hardest part of the main walk is the first few yards. Having gone through the gate at the bridge, take the path which climbs very steeply for some 30 feet, following the right side of a fence. The gradient soon eases considerably and the path leads through the woodland to emerge onto more open ground high above the first gorge. The river itself is often hidden by foliage but there are charming views over the trees and loch to the surrounding hills. Continue to follow the west bank to the upper gorge or as far as desired. Return the same way.

Maximum distance: 4 miles, allow 2 – 3 hours

31 ASCENT OF BEINN BHAN 2938ft/ 896m

B einn Bhan *'white hill' (bynvan)* is a steep sandstone mountain with an impressive line of cliff-girt, east facing corries which stretch for nearly 5 miles across the remote Applecross Peninsula. *This invigorating ascent should not be undertaken lightly. In hillfog, high winds or under winter conditions, this is no place for the inexperienced.* Easier options allow something of the majesty of the mountain to be appreciated without climbing the challenging upper sections.

P ark at Tornapress on the Applecross Road near the bridge over the River Kishorn, close to the junction with the A896. Follow the excellent path starting on the west bank by the bridge. It rises gently above the river giving fine views towards Beinn Damh and glimpses of Beinn Bhan's wild corries high above. After 1.5 miles, the path crosses the first of the streams issuing from Coire na Poite. The route runs parallel with the river for a short time. As it begins to swing away, a cairn marks the start of an intermittent and poor path climbing above the north bank. Frequent intruding sandstone provides dry relief from the wetter moorland. A pretty series of small waterfalls contrast well with the rocky grandeur above. Coire na Poite is the most imposing of the five corries. The sandstone terraced spurs of A' Chioch and A' Poite dwarf the small lonely lochan at their foot. There are several ascent routes possible from here.

In good weather, very experienced scramblers with route finding ability can tackle A' Chioch on the left. Work a way up onto the entertaining rocky ridge from a point some 600 yards south of the lochan. Beyond a broad shoulder, the ridge steepens and the easiest ground is to the left. Eventually the ridge becomes a narrow level pavement. An easy scramble then brings a dip below a steep rise. Follow the indistinct path for about 20 feet then scramble directly up the loose rock and vegetation. Regain the main ridge and follow the narrow airy crest. Where it broadens out once more, keep right and work a way round to the narrow dip below the final steep pull. The angle averages 60 degrees and there is some loose rock. A direct attack is easiest. Halfway up, a very steep rock wall is breached by an obvious chimney lying a short way to the right along a grassy ledge. Easier, though

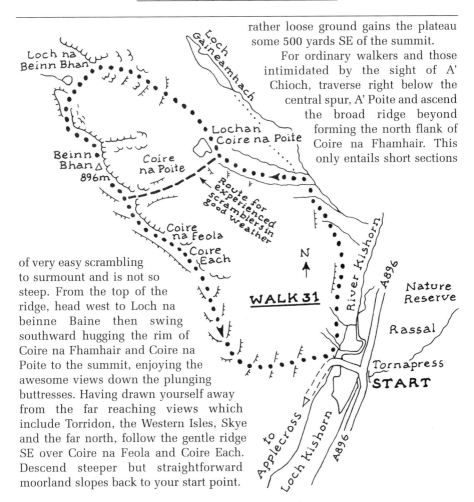

rather loose ground gains the plateau some 500 yards SE of the summit. For ordinary walkers and those intimidated by the sight of A' Chioch, traverse right below the central spur, A' Poite and ascend the broad ridge beyond forming the north flank of Coire na Fhamhair. This only entails short sections of very easy scrambling to surmount and is not so steep. From the top of the ridge, head west to Loch na beinne Baine then swing southward hugging the rim of Coire na Fhamhair and Coire na Poite to the summit, enjoying the awesome views down the plunging buttresses. Having drawn yourself away from the far reaching views which include Torridon, the Western Isles, Skye and the far north, follow the gentle ridge SE over Coire na Feola and Coire Each. Descend steeper but straightforward moorland slopes back to your start point.

FACT FILE
Route 1 Distance: 8 miles Height gain 950m/3118ft Grade 3–4 scrambling
(Route 2: 8.75 miles, 900m/2954ft)
Time: 6 – 6.5 hours
Start/Finish: Tornapress GR 834423 OS Sheet 24
Stalking: Applecross Estate, Tel. Stalkers 01520 744247 or 733249

EASIER OPTIONS
Take the aforementioned path from the bridge at Tornapress and continue along it to its end at Loch Gaineamhach: an easy ascent of *290m / 952ft in 2.5 miles* with lovely views across the wide glen towards the Torridon mountains and south to Loch Kishorn. It also allows one to enjoy the upper sections of Beinn Bhan's corries. *Allow 2.5 – 3 hours*

For an even better appreciation of the corries, follow the route as per the ascent of Beinn Bhan as far as Lochan Coire na Poite. Head north over the slabby flat moorland past the lochan then descend easily to Loch Gaineamhach. Follow the stalkers' path back down to the start. *6 miles, 350m / 1149ft, 4 hours.*

The **Rassal Nature Reserve** on the A896, a mile north of the junction with the Applecross road, also provides for short and easy walking. It is the most northerly ash wood in the country. Sallows and hazels also grow on the limestone outcrops.

32 INTO THE HEART OF APPLECROSS

The northern half of the Applecross Peninsula consists of wild, lonely moorland studded with lochans and attractive tumbling streams looking out to the Western Isles, Torridon and the far north. The tiny population clings to the coastal fringes leaving the interior uninhabited save for large deer herds and a variety of birds and visited by few. This linear walk ventures into the heart of this area making use of good paths and tracks with an optional short climb onto Croic-bheinn (493m/1618ft), an excellent viewpoint.

The walk relies on making use of the *once daily* Shieldaig – Applecross 4 seater postbus (*Mon – Sat*). It can be tackled from either end but it is probably safer to catch the postbus first to Applecross (unless staying there) then walk back to your car which should be left parked at Inverbain above Loch Shieldaig. The small village of Applecross stands in a delightful setting looking out over a shallow bay to the majestic Cuillin mountains of Skye. The walk begins at the head of the bay, on the north side of the road bridge over the River Applecross. An excellent, gentle track leads north westward through the glen. The first mile passes the delightful grounds of Applecross House where the wild rhododendrons, gorse and mature mixed woodland form a beautiful surround to the wide river. Approaching the Adventure School, enclosed fields of deer can be seen on the left. Further up the valley, wild herds roam free. Throughout much of the first 4 miles, there is a fine prospect back to Skye past the streams which have deeply incised the moorland hills. Birds include the cuckoo, heard surprisingly far up the glen, the lesser redpoll and goldcrest in the small coniferous plantations and buzzards, snipe and wheatears on the open moorland.

After 3 miles the track ends at a junction of two paths and a bridge.

Hartfield
Adventure
School

START

Applecross
House

Applecross
Bay

▽ to
Applecross

River Applecross

FINISH

Inverbain

Waterfalls

N

WALK 32

Allt an t-Srathain

Croic-
bheinn
493 m

Take the left fork climbing steadily above a major river tributary with views to the distant cliff-girt Coire Attadale below Beinn Bhan. After 400 yards, the stream cascades down through a steep defile, over a long series of pretty falls, not easily seen unless you leave the path slightly. Eas nan Cuinneag Falls translate as the 'fall of the buckets' owing to the many potholes created by the river action. At a path junction in a further mile, on the far side of a burn , bear right beside the burn under the southern flanks of Croic-bheinn. In a further 600 yards the foot of the broad south ridge of this hill is reached. This offers the easiest line of ascent to the trig point perched above the precipitous northern and western slopes. Vistas extend over the lochan spattered moorland to the Western Isles, Torridon and the distant hills of Assynt. For those electing to avoid this extra climb, another path junction is soon reached. Turn left still following the stream. Beyond a broad pass, the path now descends easily to Inverbain above the Allt an t-Srathain, passing more waterfalls with delightful views out across Loch Shieldaig and Upper Loch Torridon.

FACT FILE
Distance: 8.5 miles Height gain: 1218ft / 371m Time: 4 – 5 hours
(with Croic-bheinn 10.25 miles, 1618ft / 493m Time: 5 – 6 hours)
Start: Applecross Bay GR 714457 Finish: Inverbain GR786549 OS Sheet 24
Stalking: Applecross Estate Stalker tel. 01520 733249 or 755268
Public Transport: At present Postbus leaves Applecross 0920 arrive Shieldaig 1010, departs Shieldaig 11.30 arrives Applecross 1300 (but check locally in case of changes)

EASY OPTION
The first mile or so of the above walk from Applecross makes for a very easy and pleasant stroll. This could be combined with a visit to the walled garden at **Applecross House** which is *open during the summer.*

33 TOSCAIG CIRCULAR

This short walk explores some of the enchanting small coves in the quiet south west corner of the Applecross Peninsula and enjoys frequent and extensive views of Skye, Raasay and the smaller isles of the Inner Sound. It is particularly magical on a long, fine summer evening. The first part is easy and on good paths, suitable for everyone. The optional circular extension is surprisingly rough and complex for such low ground and is only recommended for sure-footed walkers with the ability to navigate. Several short cuts to the road are given in case you are caught out by approaching darkness.

Drive south from Applecross Village towards Toscaig. Park at the large lay-by beside the junction for Ard-dhubh, just beyond the houses at Culdie. Walk along the Ard-dhubh road for about 300 yards. The narrow, sandy shallow bay of Poll Creadha is a quiet anchorage and home to grey herons, sandpipers and numerous waders. Bear left onto an obvious track climbing gently over moorland. It soon descends to a slight dip with a burn. Seals often congregate in the tiny cove to the right. From a small rise beyond, there is the first of many views to the islands and a pretty inlet fronting the houses of Ardban. These can be reached by a good path which turns off to the right and leads around the far side of the inlet. The main track continues southward through a birch lined defile. Beyond another short rise, the route descends slightly through sheep grazing land where a few boggy patches may be encountered. The two intact houses at Coillegillie stand amongst a number of sad ruins looking out to much of Skye.

Those just wishing an easy stroll should now retrace their steps. The circular route continues above the rocky shore, making use of the sheep tracks. On reaching a craggy terrace forming a small dip, scramble easily down about 50 yards inland of the shore. Gain the sheep tracks on the far side of a large patch of flag iris, climbing through birch woodland just above the sea. Follow these to a gate in the deer fence ahead. From here there are several alternatives. Without going through the gate, ascend NE over the pathless rough, knoll covered moorland to the trig point on the unnamed hill at 114m (GR707387). This provides continuing vistas of the islands, Upper Toscaig and the houses overlooking Poll Creadha bay. From the summit head NE to a dip (GR711389). By turning right here and following the deer fence downhill, the road can be reached in a few minutes. Turn left onto the road and follow it back to the start point. *(Hill 114m would be a superb location from which to watch the sunset. This route would give the quickest way up and down when daylight is short. Allow 20 minutes up from the roadside, 15 down. Park by the nearby phone box on the road towards Toscaig).* The longer alternative from the dip would be to continue NE over the moorland back to your car.

An alternative route from the gate in the deer fence above Coillegillie, reaches the road at Toscaig Harbour in about 10 minutes. Go through the gate and follow the fence to the left. Where it turns a corner, continue straight on, descending into a grassy and flowery bowl holding a small lochan. In evening light, the new Skye bridge shows well beyond Loch Toscaig. On reaching another deer fence, turn right and follow it down through boggy birch wood. Follow the next fence again to the right to a gate near the harbour road. This leads back to the start point in 1.25 miles.

FACT FILE
Distance: variable, maximum 4 miles with maximum height gain approx. 600 ft/182m
Time: full circuit 2 - 3 hours, to Coillegillie return, 1 – 1.5 hours
Start/Finish: Junction of road to Toscaig and Ard-dhubh GR 714398 OS Sheet 24

34 THE SHIELDAIG PENINSULA

This short walk explores the quiet, roadless headland, north of the village of Shieldaig on beautiful Upper Loch Torridon. There are new and entrancing coastal and mountain vistas at every turn. Binoculars are very useful. The loch is a popular haunt for seals. I saw three pairs playfully courting close to shore. For the first time, I spied a cuckoo rather than just hearing its call. With patience, numerous birds from a variety of habitats can be enjoyed. There is a clear path throughout, though occasionally it is rough underfoot with slabs and natural rock steps to negotiate. The sandstone gives a good grip however and is rarely greasy.

Park near the war memorial in Shieldaig, just off the A896. Walk straight ahead for 100 yards past the school. Just beyond a seat, turn right onto a narrow path which climbs for a short way at right angles to the shore. This leads to a track by the school playing field. Turn left onto the obvious path, ignoring the one signed for Rubha Lodge. The route rises and falls gently above the pretty, wooded, rocky shore, beneath a series of rough knolls. A cairn marks a path junction. Keep straight on and in a further 100 yards, keep left at another junction. Over a short rise, the delightful secluded beach of Camas an Leim comes into view, down to the right. Ignore the paths bearing right towards the beach. Keep left over another small rise. Dramatic Beinn Alligin and Liathach dominate the prospect over Upper Loch Torridon. A fish farm lies close to shore.

The path continues over moorland and slabby sandstone pavements towards a trig point on a small hill, before veering to the right around its base. A short descent brings the white washed cottage of Bad-callda which has to be supplied by boat. From the cottage, look left over the sheep grazing land. About 75 yards from the shore, a rocky path rises up through the stand of birch. It crosses a short stretch

81

of moorland before it descends a little rocky staircase to another isolated house, close to the tip of the headland, looking out to the very rocky coast around Diabaig. The path now heads southward with excellent views towards the Applecross Peninsula. It leads to the cairn passed earlier. Rejoin the outward route back to Shieldaig.

FACT FILE
Distance: 2.5 miles with approximately 250 feet of ascent, 1.25 - 1.75 hours
Start/ Finish: Shieldaig GR816544 OS Sheet 24
Public Transport: Shieldaig - Strathcarron postbus connects with Inverness to Kyle trains

35 THE ASCENT OF BEINN DAMH 2957ft/ 902m

' S tag mountain' is a shapely Corbett (*pronounced byn dav*) rising steeply and dramatically on all fronts. It offers a relatively quiet ascent, away from the main crowds on the neighbouring Torridon Munros, with superb views from its 2.25 mile long whaleback ridge and plenty of floral and fluvial interest en route. The best approach begins at Annat on the shores of Loch Torridon and follows the excellent path above the Allt Coire Roill ravine (as per the start of **walk 36**).

H aving reached the path junction just above the fine waterfall, you have the choice of route. Inexperienced walkers and non scramblers are advised to take the right fork which zig zags up to the col under the NW ridge. This is then followed to the summit. This is the easiest line of ascent and descent. In clear conditions however, the more interesting ascent takes the left fork and continues on the path climbing easily below the tiered eastern cliffs and gullies to the pass of Drochaid Coire Roill. The flowery moorland over which it passes is home to innumerable orchids and small clusters of the rare white lousewort.

From the lochan at the pass, initially climb SW up the rocky ridge before turning westward and scrambling steeply up a buttress to gain the short NE ridge leading to the main quartzite summit of Beinn Damh. Any difficulties encountered en route by non scramblers can be avoided on the left. The cairn stands dramatically on the fringe of the broken eastern cliffs.

The excellent panoramas include most of the other Torridon giants and those of the Coulin Forest, Applecross and the Monar Forest. Skye shows well over the Sound of Raasay. One can continue to enjoy the vistas as the path along the narrow NW ridge is followed. The walking is straightforward though rough with the quartzite blocks gradually giving way to the sandstone boulders. The next two lesser summits can be avoided by keeping to the path on the western flanks. From the broad pass under the main summit massif, the path can be followed down to the Allt Coire Roill.

If time and energy permits, it is worthwhile delaying the descent and continuing along the ridge to the most northerly top. The narrowing ridge hugs the rim of the crags above Loch Damh. Beyond a minor top, the route descends easily to another col from where one can scramble directly onto Sgurr na Bana Mhoraire. Alternatively, an easier angled rocky path ascends the NW side. Your reward is a magnificent prospect across Upper Loch Torridon. Retrace your steps to the main col.

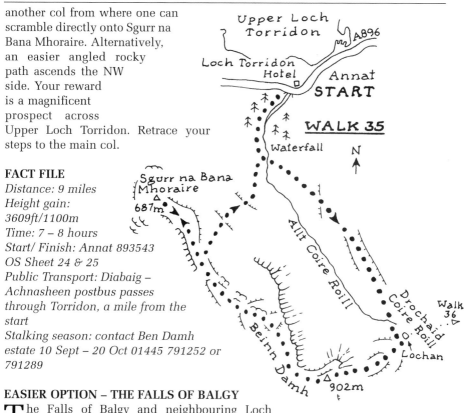

FACT FILE
Distance: 9 miles
Height gain:
3609ft/1100m
Time: 7 – 8 hours
Start/ Finish: Annat 893543
OS Sheet 24 & 25
Public Transport: Diabaig –
Achnasheen postbus passes
through Torridon, a mile from the
start
Stalking season: contact Ben Damh
estate 10 Sept – 20 Oct 01445 791252 or
791289

EASIER OPTION – THE FALLS OF BALGY

The Falls of Balgy and neighbouring Loch Damh, lie attractively in the shadow of the craggy western flanks of Beinn Damh and Ben Shieldaig. They are easily reached by a gentle stroll from the A896, about 2.5 miles east of Shieldaig village above Upper Loch Torridon. There is limited parking by the road bridge over the wide river at Balgy. Just east of the bridge, a gate gives access to a path. This follows the east bank of the river above a small birch lined gorge. In about 600 yards, the twin falls are reached; a noted salmon leap tumbling over sandstone terracing. The path continues gently to the nearby loch where a good track is joined. This can be followed above the eastern shore for up to 4 miles. Retrace your steps when desired.

Another attractive possibility is to follow the easy 3 mile track along the wooded shore of Upper Loch Torridon from the Loch Torridon Hotel at Annat to Balgy. Return the same way.

36 CIRCUIT OF BEINN NA H-EAGLAISE

This circular valley walk ventures into the wild mountainous hinterland south of Upper Loch Torridon; a region of stark and dramatic Torridonian sandstone peaks and innumerable dark lochans. The first section follows an extremely attractive river gorge; impressive even if the river is not in spate. Botanists can enjoy a feast of bog loving plants, including a variety of marsh orchids, the early purple, common spotted and heath spotted orchids, starry saxifrage and the rare white lousewort (which I've only previously seen on St Kilda) amidst the infinitely more common pink variety. With the exception of the short pathless central section, the route uses good paths with very little bog. It provides an ideal outing when high winds make mountain tops uninviting.

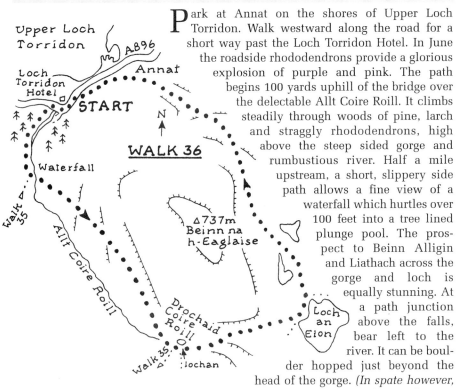

Park at Annat on the shores of Upper Loch Torridon. Walk westward along the road for a short way past the Loch Torridon Hotel. In June the roadside rhododendrons provide a glorious explosion of purple and pink. The path begins 100 yards uphill of the bridge over the delectable Allt Coire Roill. It climbs steadily through woods of pine, larch and straggly rhododendrons, high above the steep sided gorge and rumbustious river. Half a mile upstream, a short, slippery side path allows a fine view of a waterfall which hurtles over 100 feet into a tree lined plunge pool. The prospect to Beinn Alligin and Liathach across the gorge and loch is equally stunning. At a path junction above the falls, bear left to the river. It can be boulder hopped just beyond the head of the gorge. *(In spate however, the river may be difficult to cross and you may need to continue following the west bank to the pass).* The path dog-legs back a little alongside the river, before climbing away onto the gentle, flowery moorland below Beinn na h Eaglaise and the high broken imposing cliffs of Beinn Damh's eastern flanks.

At the head of the pass, Drochaid Coire Roill, the view opens out to the Coulin Forest Munros and to distant Loch Carron. A short way beyond a small lochan, leave the path and head due eastward across the rough but straightforward heather and bouldery moorland, beneath the southern flanks of Beinn na h Eaglaise. In 0.75 mile, lonely Loch an Eion is reached, dominated by the craggy sandstone terraces of domed Maol Chean-dearg and the grey scree riddled Sgorr Ruadh. Turn left at the small loch onto an excellent path which leads easily back down to Annat in a further 3 miles. The views along and across Glen Torridon cannot fail to impress. Liathach and Beinn Alligin are seen at their best if descending on a fine summer's evening when the red sandstone almost glows and every magnificent soaring buttress, pinnacle and riven gully is clearly etched.

FACT FILE
Distance: 8 miles 1444ft / 440m of ascent
Time: 4.5 – 5.5 hours
Start/ Finish: Annat 893543 OS Sheet 24 & 25
Public Transport: Diabaig – Achnasheen postbus passes through Torridon, a mile from the start
Stalking season: contact Ben Damh estate 10 Sept - 20 Oct 01445 791252 or 791289

EASIER OPTION
For those not wishing to make the full circuit, the first and last part of the walk are worthy of exploration. They are on good paths with plenty of scenic and botanical interest. Note that the final section reaches the road in Annat by a footpath sign for 'Coulags, 10 miles'.

---

37 ASCENT OF BEINN ALLIGIN 985m/ 3232ft

The Torridon mountains are among the finest in Britain. The traverse of the Beinn Alligin horseshoe is a classic and cannot fail to bring out the superlatives. The *'jewelled mountain'* is bounded on all sides by brutally steep grassy flanks, lavishly braided in rocky tiers of sandstone, crowned by airy ridges and shapely peaks and pinnacles. The magnificence of the mountain itself is matched by the outstanding views it brings. Under snow it becomes even more spectacular. In such conditions however, the traverse takes on an alpine character, suitable only for very experienced walkers.

From the Coire Mhic Nobuil car park on the road to Diabaig, a fairly obvious peaty path (unmarked on map) climbs gently north then NE over moorland before swinging west into Coir nan Laogh. The going is inclined to be boggy after rain but improves with height. The path becomes better defined and more eroded near the narrow ribbon of the Altan Glas stream. The growing vista of Upper Loch Torridon is one to saviour. Beyond the precipitous craggy corrie walls girdling Tom na Gruagaich (*town na grooageech*), the rugged peaks of the Coulin Forest and Liathach are finely arrayed. The path becomes drier and grassier as it ascends the headwall of the narrow corrie; a real suntrap in fine weather. This is no time for sunbathing however: the summit of Tom na Gruagaich lies just above. The view from here is nothing short of sensational. Vertigo sufferers would be advised to steer clear, although a paraglide-ist would feet totally at home! The NE face

plunges abruptly and giddily away beneath your feet, into the boggy depths of Toll a' Mhadaidh. The complexities of Beinn Alligin are in themselves stunning. The other Torridons and mountains of the Fisherfield and Flowerdale Forests catch the eye. On a clear day, the Inner Hebrides also vie for your attention. You may be lucky enough to see buzzards or eagles circling apparently effortlessly around the high tops; quartering the ground in their search for prey. You will almost feel like an eagle yourself, on such a lofty perch.

Try and concentrate on your feet rather than the views, as you descend a narrow, rocky ridge northward. There is an opportunity for a little easy scrambling if so desired. Beyond a knoll, moderate grassy slopes lead up a broadening ridge to the main summit, Sgurr Mhor (*skoor voar*). Just below the summit lies the head of a spectacular 500 foot vertical gash, chopped out of the southern flanks of the mountain; as though some giant has gone berserk with a meat cleaver. Sgurr Mhor actually has a lesser known but far more apposite alternative name, Sgurr na Tuaigh, *'peak of the hatchet'*.

If you can drag yourself away from another breathtaking panorama, take the good path dropping steeply down another fine narrow, rocky ridge, to reach the foot of Na Rathanan, the *'Horns of Alligin'*. Under summer conditions, the three rocky towers involve no more than delightful, easy scrambling, interspersed with walking along a distinct path. Under snow however, it could be decidedly tricky. One can spend some time picking out weird and interesting shapes in the sandstone crags or gawping at the majestic array of Liathach's northern corries across the deep glen. Alternatively, count the lochs and lochans on view: I gave up after 30!

Beinn Alligin should certainly live up to all your expectations. The descent from the final horn is thoroughly enjoyable; even for those who suffer from jippy knees. Some of the step downs are rather big but 'bottom gear' ensures a comfortable ride! Eventually the gradient becomes gentle over the moorland and leads to the Allt a' Bhealaich; an attractive stream of numerous falls, even in times of drought. This river flows into the Abhainn Coire Mhic Nobuil from where an excellent path leads back to the car park. After heavy rain, the cascades below perform a white water spectacular.

FACT FILE

Distance: 6.5 miles with 1210m/ 3970ft of ascent
Time: 6 – 8 hours
Start / Finish: National Trust car park GR 869576 OS Sheet 24 or 1:25,000
Torridon/Skye map
Remarks: a serious expedition in winter, for experts only
Stalking season: no restrictions, NTS property
Public Transport: Achnasheen – Diabaig postbus passes start

EASIER OPTION – see **walk 38** Coire Mhic Nobuil

38 COIRE MHIC NOBUIL

The path which follows the boisterous Abhainn Coire Mhic Nobuil beneath the northern flanks of Liathach in Torridon, provides a relatively easy walk full of dramatic, scenic interest. For those just desirous of a short walk, (or in wet weather) it is very rewarding just following the path for a mile then retracing one's steps. The more energetic can walk through the entire valley. By catching the postbus either at the start or finish of the day, you will avoid a long road walk.

Start at the National Trust car park beside the river, some 2.5 miles west of Torridon village on the road to Diabaig. From the road bridge, the largest of the waterfalls along the river's course, can be seen 100 yards away. The striking gorge is enclosed by old Scots pine, beneath the rugged ramparts of Beinn Alligin. The easy to follow path climbs gently through the woodland to emerge in the open glen between Beinn Alligin and Liathach. The main path itself is usually fairly dry underfoot. However, to see the best of the small, rocky river gorge, it is worth braving the various short, boggy side paths to the left. There are a succession of small falls, rapids and pot holes with views back to Loch Torridon. The path continues

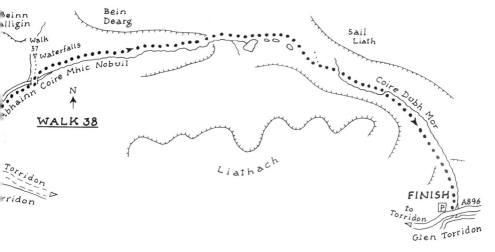

for about a mile just above the south bank before crossing a bridge and following a tributary upstream for 200 yards. This too has pretty waterfalls with the rock towers, the Horns of Alligin forming a dramatic backcloth. At the path junction, turn right and continue up the glen following the north bank of the Abhainn Coire Mhic Nobuil. The broken cliffs and precipitous grassy flanks of Beinn Dearg rear up to the left, whilst the magnificent pinnacled and cliff-girt corries of Liathach fill the view to the right. Towards the eastern end of the mountain, turn right at a junction, to pick up the rough, bouldery path descending Coire Dubh Mor. It descends easily between the impressive crags of the eastern top of Liathach and the huge scree riddled western flanks of Sail Liath. The National Trust car park in upper Glen Torridon is reached in 2.5 miles. The postbus will avoid a 7 – 8 mile return walk along the glen or road.

FACT FILE
Distance: 8 miles with height gain 1378ft/ 420m Time: 4 – 5 hours
Start: GR 869576 OS Sheet 24 Finish: GR 959569 OS Sheet 25
Achnasheen – Diabaig Postbus currently passes finish approx 14.05 hours (Mon – Sat) but check with the local Tourist Information Centre or Post Office

39 DIABAIG CIRCULAR

This walk enjoys ever-changing views as it explores the wild and beautiful coast above Loch Diabaig and Loch Torridon. There is a clear path throughout, though it is occasionally rough underfoot with boulders and easy rocky staircases. It can be shortened by using the postbus between Alligan Shuas and Diabaig, saving several miles of road walking. The walk is described anti clockwise, starting from Diabaig, though is just as easily reversed depending on whether you prefer to road walk or catch a bus. At the time of writing, the bus leaves Diabaig at *09.55 hours, returning in late afternoon* (check with Post Offices in the area to confirm times).

The peaceful harbour at Diabaig looks out to Skye, Applecross and the Outer Hebrides, beyond the sheltering horseshoe of rugged grey sandstone hills. Follow the harbour southward. Beyond the last house, a path climbs steeply between crags, popular with rock climbers. The cliffs contrast sharply with the alder and birch woodland, springtime lambs and flower filled gardens below. The shimmering waters of Loch Diabaig are now a hive of fish farming activity. This 400 foot ascent is the stiffest of the day. The route now descends easily for 100 feet before climbing steadily for 200 feet onto lochan studded rocky moorland. (Ignore the path bearing off to your right near the start of the climb). The path descends gently between rocky knolls past Loch a Bhealaich Mhoir, a delightful spot on a sunny day and when the waterlilies are in flower. A small rise leads to another delectable lochan, Lochan Dubh. Just below here, one comes to the best views of the day. A remote whitewashed cottage lies amidst a grassy sward above the rocky cove of Port Laire. The rugged, shapely peaks of Beinn Damh, Maol Chean-dearg and Beinn Bhann provide the striking backcloth.

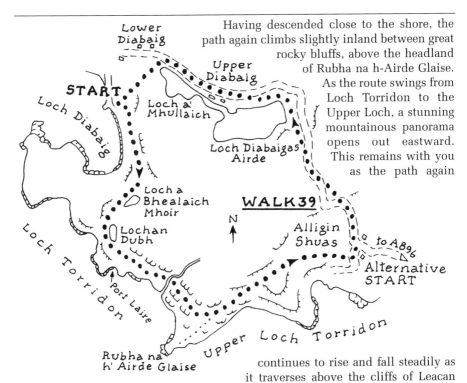

Having descended close to the shore, the path again climbs slightly inland between great rocky bluffs, above the headland of Rubha na h-Airde Glaise. As the route swings from Loch Torridon to the Upper Loch, a stunning mountainous panorama opens out eastward. This remains with you as the path again continues to rise and fall steadily as it traverses above the cliffs of Leacan Bana. Keep straight on at a path junction, ignoring the path bearing right. At a second junction, about 800 yards on, keep left. This contours above the houses of Alligin Shuas to meet the road just above the hamlet (an alternative start point for the walk).

If not catching the postbus, turn left uphill and left again at another road junction in 300 yards. The quiet highway to Diabaig climbs steeply with continuing fine vistas behind across Upper Loch Torridon. In 500 yards, just before some bad hairpin bends, one can take a short cut footpath on the right, leading to the head of the road. Having rejoined the road for a few hundred yards, you may like to take the next shortcut, this time on the left, just after two tiny lochans. The path descends easily to the NE corner of Loch Diabaigas Airde where there is an awkward manœurvre around a fence which projects into the loch. Thereafter it easily crosses fields to rejoin the road above the north shore by a ruined croft. Continue along the road for a further mile until the northern corner of Loch a' Mhullaich. Turn left off the road along the north shore, go through a gate then follow the indistinct path steeply down to the finish at Diabaig. This keeps the lively Allt an Uain burn to the right and a fence to your left.

FACT FILE
Distance: 7.5 miles, 1500ft/ 457m of ascent, 5 hours
Start/ Finish: Diabaig GR 797597 or Alligin Shuas GR 831580 OS Sheet 24

40 DIABAIG TO REDPOINT

There is no road for the 7 miles between Diabaig and Redpoint on the northern shore of Loch Torridon. A clear path stretches the whole way and makes for easy and highly scenic walking. Unfortunately, public transport is insufficient to allow a one way walk. One must walk for as far as desired from either end and then return.

When descending the steep road into Diabaig, turn left to the western end of the village, away from the road running down to the harbour. The cairned path starts from the road end and traverses the gentle, flowery cliff tops below Sidhein a' Mhill some 300 feet above the sea. The going is initially inclined to be a bit boggy. After 2 miles a short steep descent brings you to Craig Youth Hostel, one of the remotest in the country. Having crossed the birch fringed River Craig, the path continues to Redpoint, gently undulating just above the sea. The rocky shore eventually gives way to sandy beaches and dunes. Throughout there are absorbing views to the Outer Hebrides, to the Cuillins and Trotternish hills of Skye, to Applecross and Raasay. Binoculars are useful, as Loch Torridon is a haven for seals, colonies of seabirds and otters, whilst inland, feral goats roam freely.

If starting from Redpoint, this is reached by a minor road just south of Gairloch. On a fine day this is an enchanting place with bays of bright red sand backed by large dunes, cliffs and heather moorland. These beaches are safe for bathing. There is a car park at the road end with a cairn and viewpoint indicator.

FACT FILE *Distance optional, maximum 14 miles, 6 – 8 hours*
Start/Finish: either Diabaig GR 788606 or Redpoint GR732688 OS Sheet 24

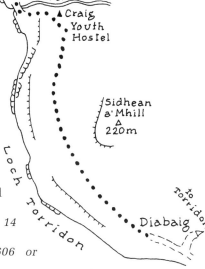

41 THE TRAVERSE OF LIATHACH

Liathach *(leeagach)* is a massive Leviathan. Its two quartzite Munro summits stand atop precipitous tiered sandstone flanks abutted by craggy buttresses and riven by deep gullies. From the road it looks as impregnable as a medieval castle. For the experienced walker, its traverse is one of the classic expeditions of the Highlands, worth saving for a fine day.

About 800 yards east of Glen Cottage in Glen Torridon, a well defined path climbs steeply beside the Allt an Doire Ghairbh, an attractive stream with falls and deep narrow gorges along part of its course. Violets, butterworts, thrift and eyebright provide a welcome splash of colour amongst the forbidding towering walls of grass, scree and crags of the Toll a' Meith. Somehow the path wends through the maze of crags without encountering any real difficulties (in summer conditions).

From a col at 833m / 2733 ft, the route continues westward over Stob a' Coire Liath Mhor. In thick mist some sections of route could be confusing as the path picks a way over rough quartzite rubble and round wee outcrops. Even if the far mountains are lost in haze, those near at hand will impress hugely: stark, shapely and dramatic. On a clear day vistas can extend from Ben Hope in the far north to Ben Nevis. The last 100 feet onto the summit of the first Munro involve an entertaining clamber over large boulders. From Spidean a'Choire Leith 3456ft/1054m *'peak of the grey corrie' (speedyan a chora lyayha)*, the rest of Liathach is a stunning sight. This is particularly true looking westward to magnificent Coire na Caime and the attendant peaks of Mullach an Rathain and Meall Dearg. The tiny deep-set lochans of this great bowl are overshadowed by a huge headwall buttressing the Am Fasarinen pinnacles; a vast natural cathedral.

Continuing towards Am Fasarinen, it is easy to lose the path amidst the jumble of boulders which require care to cross. The path eventually splits. One can choose to scramble over the exposed and spectacular shattered sandstone pinnacles on good clinging rock or take the avoiding path on the south side. The latter keeps meeting up with the pinnacles route at tiny cols, enabling non scramblers to admire the massive cliffs plunging into the depths of Coire na Caime. The routes only really diverge around Am Fasarinen itself. The path may lack the scrambling but is equally spectacular, being very narrow and exposed with a long drop to the

River Torridon and Glen Cottage. At one point the path has broken away completely necessitating a cautious clamber along steep grass above the drop. In numerous other places it is beginning to disintegrate and eventually the path could become unusable forcing one to scramble the pinnacles. Beyond the pinnacles an easy ridge walk brings the summit of the second Munro, Mullach an Rathain 3358ft/1023m, *'summit of the row of pinnacles' (mooloch an rahan)* and hopefully a delectable view of shimmering Upper Loch Torridon and Hebridean islands.

The descent is equally as steep as the ascent. Turn down the south west ridge for 200 yards and take the path into the Toll Ban, following the Allt an Tuill Bhain. A walking stick is very useful for negotiating the mixture of very steep sandy scree and boulders. After some 800 feet, the sand gives way to grass, heather and slippery peat. A fine view to the peaks of the Coulin Forest dominate much of the descent until the lower slopes are reached awash in beautiful orchids. The path finishes at the road 1.5 miles west of the start. The walk back allows a leisurely appreciation of Liathach's awesome ramparts, something that is difficult to do whilst driving up the glen.

FACT FILE
Distance: 5.5 miles Height gain: 4100ft/1249m
Time: 6 – 8 hours
Start: Glen Torridon GR 937566 Finish: GR 921557 OS Sheet 25
Remarks: Under winter conditions a major expedition only for experienced mountaineers. In summer, inexperienced walkers are advised to go with a guide, contact NTS Ranger 01445 791221
Stalking: no access restrictions NTS Property
Public Transport: post bus along Glen Torridon connects with buses and trains at Achnasheen

EASIER OPTION see **walk 38**

42 THE ASCENT OF SGORR NAN LOCHAN UAINE 2865ft/ 873m & SGURR DUBH 2566ft/ 782m

On a typical weekend, hordes of walkers flock to the giant Torridon Munros to enjoy the imposing sandstone terracing, wild corries, airy ridges and stunning views. Being amongst the finest hills in Britain, this attention is deserved. However, the mountains forming part of the south side of the glen, are, unjustly, sadly neglected. Although lower, their ascent is equally challenging and rewarding ,with the bonus of seclusion. They are worth saving for a fine day; for the stunning panoramas and *to avoid a navigational headache.*

Across the road from the Coire Dubh car park at the eastern end of Liathach in Glen Torridon, a good stalkers' path begins at the nearby bridge and skirts round reedy Lochan an Isgair to reach the Ling Hut. The scene is dominated by the impressive and seemingly impregnable bulk of Liathach and huge scree runs of Beinn Eighe. Beyond the hut and an attractive stream, the path climbs gradually

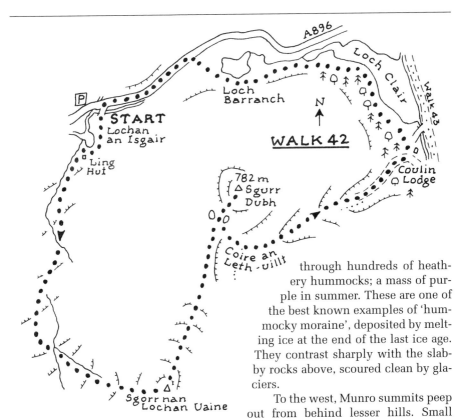

through hundreds of heathery hummocks; a mass of purple in summer. These are one of the best known examples of 'hummocky moraine', deposited by melting ice at the end of the last ice age. They contrast sharply with the slabby rocks above, scoured clean by glaciers.

To the west, Munro summits peep out from behind lesser hills. Small lochans abound and eventually Upper Loch Torridon hoves into view. Leave the path at approximately GR 953538 below the wide pass holding Lochan Uaine. Head SW towards the pass ascending the pathless but straightforward heather and boulder slopes. Just below the lochans, take a short cut onto Sgorr nan Lochan Uaine, *'peak of the little green lochan'* (*skoor na lochyn ooanya*). There is no set route, you choose one to suit your abilities. Grassy slopes become more bouldery and eventually scree, boulders and small sandstone and quartz crags predominate. It is possible to scramble a fair bit on the sound rock.

From the excellent grandstand summit platform, an extremely complex ridge connects with Sgurr Dubh, *'black peak'* (*skoor doo*) ; a navigational nightmare in mist. The route consists mainly of an erratic boulder hop, though narrow grassy corridors can often be used to work a way between the large hummocks and small crags. It is very rough and slow going and a matter of watching one's feet. Remember to stop occasionally to appreciate the superb vistas! I was lucky enough to twice spy an eagle, rising vertically on the thermals like a Harrier jet. Always a thrilling sight!

The broad col is a complex cluster of small dips, each containing tiny lochans. Work a way through these seemingly endless hollows and hillocks on Sgurr Dubh until a sizeable dip in the ridge is reached, containing the largest lochan over-looked by a series of crags beyond (GR 976554). A steep, bouldery and grassy gully cuts up between the crags just to the right of the lochan, giving access to the high-est lake. A quartzite bouldery clamber then leads to the summit cairn and an eagle's eye view down to the road in Glen Torridon, dwarfed by mighty Liathach and Beinn Eighe.

There is a choice of descent routes. The roughest and trickiest way is to head WSW to avoid a sandstone cliff, then work a way steeply down WNW through a maze of outcrops and hummocky moraine to reach the Ling Hut. Longer but sceni-cally finer and gentler, the alternative leads down to Loch Clair. Retrace your steps to the largest lochan, then descend steep but easy grass and heather slopes near a stream, to connect with the fine stalkers' path heading down from Coire an Leth-uillt. The lower valley is a delightful mix of Scots pine, holly, birch and rowan. Lousewort and milkwort paint tiny splashes of colour at your feet.

From Coulin Lodge, keep to the track on the south side of beautiful Loch Clair. Just before a large shed, some 300 yards beyond the buildings, take the scenic path forking left. This climbs slightly above the loch, through Scots pines before even-tually working its way round to Loch Bharranch. A short heather bash brings the road and in a mile the car park.

FACT FILE

Distance: 12 miles Height gain 3600ft / 1096m
Time: 7 – 9 hours
Remarks: Rough & pathless on the upper hills. Good navigation skills required in mist.
Start/ Finish: Coire Dubh Car park Glen Torridon GR 957569 OS Sheet 25
Public Transport: Diabaig – Achnasheen Post bus passes through Glen Torridon
Stalking season: Coulin Estate Stalker 01445 760383

EASY OPTION – see **Circuit of Loch Clair and Loch Coulin (walk 43)**

43 LOCH COULIN AND LOCH CLAIR

The gentle circuit of these two lochans provides one of the most beautiful walks in the north west Highlands, particularly in late May and early June when the huge banks of wild rhododendrons are in full bloom.

There is limited parking opposite the start of the private road to Coulin Lodge on the A896, some 3 miles south west of Kinlochewe (also lay-by 0.5 mile to the west). Follow the tarmac road south beside Loch Clair. The roadsides are lined with birches and rhododendrons which frame the majestic Torridon mountains perfectly. Beinn Eighe, Liathach, Sgurr Dubh and Meall an Leathaid Mhoir are all seen to good effect.

At the south end of Loch Clair, keep straight on, following the left bank of a short stretch of river. Loch Coulin is soon reached. Keep to the easy track and path along the north shore. The going is generally good underfoot with strategically placed pieces of bog wood over the occasionally marshy patch. This loch is much more open than Loch Clair with barer hill-sides beyond the more scattered trees and rhododendrons. The reedy waters are popular with waterfowl. At the far end of the loch, stalkers' ponies are usually seen grazing near Torran Cuilinn. Beyond this cottage, the path crosses the River Coulin and swings round towards Coulin Farm and the far side of the loch. Ignoring the track near the farm which bears left for Achnashellach, keep to the Land-Rover track following the south shore back towards Coulin Lodge. Halfway along, a rowing boat is often tied up on the fore-shore. With the distant massif grey bulk of multi-topped Beinn Eighe, it is a photographers delight. This shot has appeared in a number of TV and maga-zine adverts. The woodland of birch, alder and stately old Scots pine surrounding the Lodge, enhance the scene still further. Approaching the Lodge, cross the footbridge over the narrows of Loch Coulin and turn left, rejoining the outward route along Loch Clair.

FACT FILE

Distance:6 miles Time: 2.5 – 3.5 hours Virtually Flat
Start / Finish: A896 GR 003581 OS Sheet 25
Public Transport: Diabaig – Achnasheen postbus passes start, once daily Mon. – Sat.

44 THE ASCENT OF SLIOCH 3217ft / 980m

Loch Maree, guarded by fortress Slioch, is a jewel in north western Scotland's crown and justifiably attracts significant numbers of tourists annually. In good conditions, Slioch itself gives a relatively straightforward ascent with the reward of one of the finest panoramas in Scotland.

An easy undulating path follows the beautiful wooded north bank of the Kinlochewe River away from Incheril, towards the shores of Loch Maree. In late spring, fields of playful lambs echo to the calls of cuckoos. Overlooking this pastoral tranquillity, the impressive bulk of Beinn Eighe dominates. After 2.5 miles, a footbridge spans the gushing Abhainn an Fhasaigh and the path turns into crag rimmed Gleann Bianasdail. The river roars through a spectacular narrow, deeply incised gorge in a series of falls and rapids plunging into dark pools patrolled by dippers. A smattering of ancient pines survive above the gorge, enhancing the scene still further.

Some 1.5 miles of gentle ascent leads to the prominent stream flowing from the SE corrie of Slioch (shleeach). Turn up alongside its attractive falls, quite steeply at first, until over the corrie lip. Steep grassy slopes lead out of the corrie bowl, the haunt of deer and wild goats. A band of crags under the summit can be avoided by bearing right onto the eastern ridge. Only over the last few hundred yards does the gradient ease. The trig point will come as a welcome sight, although the nearby north top offers the finer viewpoint. The scene is one of

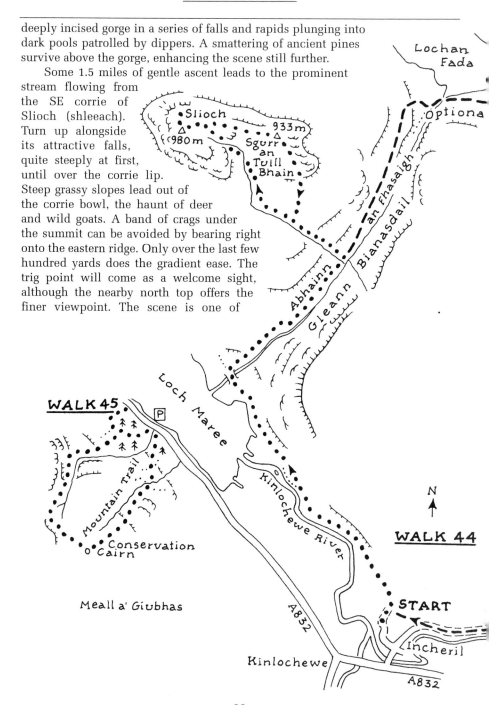

stark, rugged beauty, of nature in the raw; there is nothing gentle about the western giants of Torridon, the Fannaichs, Monar Forest and Fisherfield Forest, or the great plunging NW buttress of Slioch facing out to Loch Maree. It seems in keeping with the area's violent history. Loch Maree's 30 islands were once strongholds and hiding places for the marauding Viking galleys which ravaged the area. Later, the MacKenzies and MacRaes battled with the MacLeods, driving them from their Gairloch lands.

From the north top, a delightful narrow ridge leads to the eastern top, Sgurr an Tuill Bhain. Somewhat brutally steep grass and heather leads back down to the stream of ascent. Rather than rejoin your outward route, hardy walkers can opt for a long circular return. Having rejoined the path in Gleann Bianasdail, the way continues to the outflow of delectable, remote Lochan Fada and *a potentially dangerous river crossing that should not be attempted after heavy rain.* It had always been a mystery to me why Slioch, *'the spear'* was so named, until I visited the loch and saw the shapely point reflected in the still waters. Head ESE above the loch to pick up the excellent stalkers' path below Loch an Sgiereach. This soon widens to a Land-Rover track, allowing for brisk progress. At the Heights of Kinlochewe, the track swings SW back to Incheril. The Abhainn Bruachaig has carved out small gorges leaving well sculptured and tilted rocks with dinky falls tumbling over sandstone steps, surrounded by birches and rowans. A picturesque finish to a splendid expedition.

FACT FILE

Distance if returning by outward route: 12 miles
Height gain: 1030m/3380ft
Time: 6 – 7 hours (For circular route, 18 miles 8 – 10 hours)
Start/Finish: Small car park in Incheril by Kinlochewe GR 033626 OS Sheet 19
Public transport: Inverness to Poolewe buses stop at Kinlochewe
Stalking season: Letterewe Estate Stalker 01445 760302, usually no access except weekends 15 Sept – 15 Nov

EASY OPTION

The first part of the main walk along the Kinlochewe River to Loch Maree is extremely gentle and picturesque. Return the same way.

45 BEINN EIGHE NATURE RESERVE TRAILS

The Beinn Eighe reserve above Loch Maree was established in 1951 as Britain's first National Nature Reserve. It is home to more than 300 species of mosses and liverworts, 39 ferns and horsetail , 284 species of flowering plants, 14 different butterflies, 13 dragonflies, 423 moths and 134 spiders. The 121 recorded species of birds include the golden eagle, ptarmigan and snow bunting on the high mountains, merlin, wheatear, whinchat and golden plover on the moorland and crossbill, siskin, redstart, sparrowhawk and wood warbler in the woods. Two easy to follow trails have been laid, starting from the car park on the south shore of Loch Maree, about 2.5 miles north west of Kinlochewe. Informative trail booklets are sold from dispensing machines (also available at Aultroy Visitor Centre & Kinlochewe Garage). *Note that dogs are not allowed on the reserve.*

1 The Woodland Trail (*allow 1 hour*)
This easy 1 mile trail climbs for about 300 feet into one of the finest and few remaining fragments of the great Caledonian Forest dating back some 8000 years. Amongst the many Scots pines and birches, a few willows, alder and rowan are found. The trail initially follows what was once a rough track made for extracting timber during World War II. The large scale wartime felling continued the damage begun in the 19th century. Overgrazing by sheep and deer prevented tree regeneration. Similarly the deliberate burning which encouraged growth of the heather shoots for sheep and grouse. The re-afforestation begun in the 1960's is now almost indistinguishable from the surrounding ancient woodland.

Undergrowth of heather, blaeberry and cowberry provides food for the birds and gives ideal cover for the pine marten, fox and wildcat which inhabit the reserve. As height is gained, you are rewarded with a fine view of Slioch and Gleann Bianasdale across Loch Maree. Descending from the high point, you pass one of the biggest and oldest trees in the forest; a fine 65 feet oak specimen about 250 years old.

2 The Mountain Trail (*allow 3 – 4 hours*)
This 4 mile trail climbs to 1800 feet and is often rough and steep. Boots are essential.

The trail passes through a number of vegetation zones ranging from temperate woodland to arctic tundra. Initially the path climbs through the pine forest following the Allt na h-Airidhe, spawning ground for salmon and trout. Above the tree line around 1000 feet, the route passes over poorly drained, often rocky moorland with infertile and thin soils. Vegetation becomes increasingly stunted, a fine example of dwarf shrub heath. Sedges and mosses mingle with the heather, deergrass, prostrate juniper, mountain azalea and crowberry.

From the huge Conservation Cairn at the highpoint of 1800 feet, 31 Munro summits can be seen on a clear day. (Hillwalkers wishing to extend the climb, can easily ascend Meall a' Ghiubhais 2881ft/ 878m from this highpoint. Skirt the wee lochans west of the cairn and ascend the steep but straightforward eastern flanks of grass and boulders. From the large cairn on the south summit, the superb views include many of the northern corries of Beinn Eighe).

The Trail crosses a lunar like plateau to the Lunar Loch, actually named in commemoration of the first moon landing. In spite of the harsh habitat, frogs and palmate newts spawn here in addition to many insects. The path now descends to the sheltered and luxuriantly vegetated Allt na h-Airighe gorge. The sandstone and quartz give way to dolomitic shale; rocks which contain some of the earliest fossilised animal remains in Scotland. Being rich in lime and potassium, this rock was processed in kilns and used into this century for liming and fertilising the local agricultural land. Leaving the impressive gorge behind, the trail descends to join the top of the woodland trail. Turn left here and follow the path back to the car park.

46 COIRE MHIC FHEARCHAIR & BEINN EIGHE

This walk ascends to arguably the finest corrie in Scotland, Coire Mhic Fhearchair (*pronounced corrie veck errecher*). Lying beneath the western summits of Beinn Eighe north of Glen Torridon, a stately succession of waterfalls lead to the dark lochan set in a spectacular amphitheatre. Linked to the craggy terraces of Sail Liath, the centre piece is the Triple Buttress, the near-vertical, gully riven, 1300 foot cliffs of red sandstone topped by white quartzite. From the lochan there is an optional ascent onto the summit of Beinn Eighe. There are two equi-distant lines of approach. Both offer suitable sheltered routes in high winds. A fine expedition would be to link the two routes into one linear traverse but unfortunately this is not feasible unless in a two car party, given the lack of public transport.

The most popular route is from the Coire Dubh National Trust car park at the eastern end of Liathach in Glen Torridon. There is a distinct path the entire way. However, it is rough for much of the 5 miles with a never ending and irksome succession of boulder hopping or large, loose stones to dodge. It makes for very slow going. Scenically however, it is very enjoyable if you save it for a fine day. The path climbs steadily to 1200 feet, above the Allt a' Choire Dhuibh Mhoir, beneath the impressive crags of the eastern top of Liathach and the huge scree riddled western flanks of Sail Liath, the western top of Beinn Eighe. The going levels out for a time, with views to several of the magnificent northern corries of Liathach and the equally steep and craggy peaks of Beinn Dearg and the Flowerdale Corbetts which rear up abruptly from the surrounding boggy moorland. At a path junction, keep right. The rough, cairned route makes a rising traverse around the base of Sail Liath to meet the tumbling waters of the Allt Coire Mhic Fhearchair just below the corrie lochan.

FACT FILE
Return walk 10 miles with 1640ft/500m of ascent, 5 hours
Start/ Finish: Glen Torridon GR 959569 OS Sheets 25 & 19 or 1:25,000 Torridon/Skye map

Public Transport: *Diabaig – Achnasheen Postbus runs through Glen Torridon*

Bridge of Grudie

START WALK 46B

N.B. North is not at the top of this map

Glen

River Grudie

walk 47

Beinn a' Chearcaill

Allt Coire Mhic Fhearchain

46B Personally, I prefer the alternative route climbing through quieter Glen Grudie. Park in the vicinity of Grudie Bridge on the shores of Loch Maree, either on the rough ground beside the twin bridges or on the roadside verges. Some 300 yards to the west, an excellent path begins. It passes great banks of rhododendrons, to the immediate left of a house, before rising steadily above the wide and normally boisterous River Grudie. The attractive wide strath is dominated to the north by Slioch and southward by the multi topped complexities of Beinn Eighe. On the micro scale, innumerable moths flit amongst the colourful bog plants. This is also deer and golden eagle territory. The going is good underfoot for some 3.5 miles. The path then stops on reaching the Allt Coire Mhic Fhearchair under the craggy flanks of Beinn a' Chearcaill. Cross the river when feasible (it is usually possible to boulder hop) and make your own way south westward to the corrie over the steepening moorland.

FACT FILE
Return walk 10 miles with 1770ft/540m of ascent, 5 hours
Start/Finish: Grudie Bridge GR 963678 OS Sheet 19
Stalking season: 1 Sept – 20 Nov contact Grudie & Talladale Estate 01445 760259
Public Transport: Gairloch – Achnasheen postbus travels along Loch Maree, also Westerbus & Inverness Traction buses.

Loch Coire Mhic Fhearchair

Sail Mhor

Beinn Eighe

Coire Dubh Mor

Coire Dhuib Mhoir

Allt a' Choire

START WALK 46A [P]

N.B. North is not at the top of this map

A896 to Torridon

Walk 42

46A Having reached the corrie, Munro baggers can easily continue onto the main summit of Beinn Eighe, Ruadh Stac Mor 3309ft/1010m. Follow the lochan to its southern end. Inspite of the liberal draping of scree above the initial slopes of grass and boulders, in clear weather it is possible to find a thin, almost unbroken grassy rake which leads steeply but straightforwardly through the stony wastes. This gains the rocky ridge about 400 yards south of the summit. Rather than retrace your steps (if starting in Glen Torridon), in good conditions, head southwards along the ridge to a subsidiary top on the main ridge. You can either descend steeply south from here into the Coire Duhh Mor or continue eastward along the ridge to the top at 972m. From the trig point, take the SE ridge then turn down eastward into the Coire an Laoigh where a path can be picked up heading down to the road about 1 mile north east of the start.

11.5 miles, 3610ft/1100m of ascent, 8 hours

47 ASCENT OF BEINN A' CHEARCAILL 2397ft/ 725m

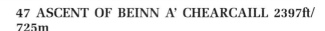

Beinn a' Chearcaill is an unfrequented hill, being neither Munro nor Corbett. This circular hillwalk however, offers varying and superb scenery, far from the madding crowds. The last section follows the Talladale Gorge, one of the north west's little known scenic gems. Navigational competence is required. Much of the route is pathless, although it is obvious in clear conditions.

Park at the finish at Talladale by Loch Maree, in a lay-by just east of the river bridge. To avoid the 3 mile road walk between here and the start at Grudie Bridge, catch the early morning postbus (*Mon – Sat*) at the Loch Maree Hotel 0.25 mile to the west of the Talladale Bridge (*currently 8.20am*) or the later service bus.

Grudie Bridge is a pretty spot with two fine old stone

WALK 47

bridges enclosed by Scots pine, looking out to the mighty ramparts of Slioch across Loch Maree. Some 300 yards to the west, an excellent path begins. It passes great banks of rhododendrons to the immediate left of a house, before rising steadily through the attractive wide strath above the wide and normally boisterous River Grudie.

About 1.5 miles along the glen, below the broken craggy flanks of Beinn a' Chearcaill, leave the path just east of the main stream issuing from Coire Briste. Head into the corrie, crossing the gentle heather and sandstone moorland above the stream. A steep but straightforward grassy headwall gains the easy upper rocky slopes of the hill. Head SW to the sandstone summit, across the large lochan spattered plateau (very confusing in mist). There are magnificent vistas across Loch Maree to the Letterewe peaks and to the cliff girt Torridon mountains. The view into the spectacular Coire Mhic Fhearchair below Beinn Eighe, is particularly striking from the summit, perched airily above a crag.

From the cairn, descend the gentle slopes northward for about a mile, then steer NW, working a way down the heathery and grassy slopes to the wide Talladale River. The going continues to be rough and pathless though deer tracks can occasionally be used to ease progress. Some 2 miles from the road, the sluggish river abruptly drops 70 feet into a spectacular gorge. This whole area used to be well wooded until the tree cover was devoured by the hungry furnaces of an ironworks at Talladale in the 17th century. The area is gradually being re-afforested. The deep-cut, steep sided gorge which extends virtually all the way to Loch Maree, is flanked by beautiful birch, oak, rowan, alder and Scots pine. Even non botanists will also enjoy the mass carpeting of milkwort, orchids, lousewort, scrub willow, heather and huge butterwort. The prospect to Beinn Airigh Charr and Loch Maree is equally enchanting. Keep to the moorland just above the gorge; a deer track runs for much of the way. Approaching an old steading, the gorge peters out and the deer track follows close to the river, alive with rapids. A broad track is joined at the dilapidated house and leads in 400 yards to the road at Talladale.

FACT FILE
Distance: 9 miles with 2313 ft / 705m of ascent
Time: 6 – 7 hours
Start: Grudie Bridge GR 963678 Finish: Talladale GR 920703 OS sheet 19
Stalking season: 1 Sept – 20 Nov contact Grudie & Talladale Estate 01445 760259
Public Transport: Gairloch – Achnasheen postbus travels along Loch Maree. Note that times can change so do check. Also Inverness Traction mid morning bus runs westward along loch & Westerbus runs eastward.

EASIER OPTIONS
The aforementioned excellent path climbing gently through Glen Grudie, offers an easy and attractive glen walk suitable for any walker. It extends for 3.5 miles. Return the same way.

The 2 mile walk up the Talladale Gorge and back is very rewarding and involves only some 700 feet of climbing. With no proper path however, it is rough underfoot unless in a dry spell and you can find the deer tracks. Only suitable for sure footed walkers.

48 THE 'TOLLIE PATH'

This scenic, relatively gentle, easy to follow path, runs for 6 miles from Tollie Farm above the northern end of Loch Maree to Slatterdale on its southern shore. It affords grand views of the loch and the surrounding mountains. A short diversion from the highpoint of the path (at 788ft/240m) onto an unnamed peak, provides greatly extended panoramas, well worth the little extra effort. The going is generally good underfoot though after heavy rain, the path is inclined to become a running stream. A number of streams have to be boulder hopped if the full walk is tackled. There are a number of options available depending on how energetic you wish to be.

For a short 2 mile stroll with very gentle climbing, park at the picnic area at Slatterdale on the shore of Loch Maree (signed from the A832 road). The path follows the shore northward for a short way then enters dense forest. In just under a mile, an excellent viewpoint is reached, looking out over the myriad of wooded islands on Loch Maree to Slioch, Beinn Airigh Charr and Beinn Eighe. Return the same way. Allow 1 hour.

For more extensive views and a 4 mile walk (with 886ft/270m of ascent), start at the Tollie Farm end. There is a good lay-by on the road just west of the farm track. The signed path for Slatterdale begins a short distance to the west, following a small river valley under craggy Creag Mhor Thollaidh. It climbs steadily to a plateau area infilled with tiny lochans, enclosed by numerous rocky sandstone hills. From the watershed highpoint, there is a picture postcard view of Loch Maree. A small pointed hill rises 263ft/80m to the immediate right of this highpoint. Sure-footed walkers who make the short and steep but easy scramble to its summit, will be rewarded with breathtaking vistas to seaward, across Loch Maree to the Torridon hills and to the shapely mountains of central Sutherland. Return the same way. *Allow 2 – 2.5 hours.*

For those wishing to walk the full path but prefer not to have to retrace one steps, start at Slatterdale around mid afternoon and aim to reach Tollie Farm by 6.45pm *(allow 3 – 3.5 hours).* On *Mon, Wed & Sat,* a Westerbus passes the finish at Tollie Farm in early evening and will return you to Slatterdale (tel. 01445 712255).
FACT FILE
6 miles, 1050ft/320m of ascent if unnamed hill included (788ft/240m if you keep to the path)
3 – 3.5 hours.

49 RUBHA REIDH & CAMAS MOR

This exhilarating coastal and short hillwalk, samples the finest part of the dramatic rocky coastline along the north side of the broad Rubha Reidh (roo a ree) peninsula. Projecting out into The Minch, it is worth saving for a good day when the islands of Skye, Harris and Lewis and much of the west Sutherland coast are clearly visible for long sections of the walk.

The public road from Gairloch running along the western side of the peninsula, ends at Melvaig, 3.5 miles south of Rubha Reidh lighthouse. Unless staying in the hostel accommodation at the lighthouse or have permission to drive up the private road, you will have to park at Melvaig just before the road end turning circle. The switchback road lies back from the cliff edges so to see the best of this coastline will require the occasional off road detour. This is easiest near the start and finish when the cliffs are nearest at hand. Particularly worthwhile are several points approaching the lighthouse. About 500 yards away as the crow flies, the road swings very close to the grassy cliff top and a 50 yard diversion brings a great view southward. Some 200 yards from the lighthouse, again leave the road and descend steeply to cross a burn. This tumbles in a significant overhanging waterfall into a small but impressive rocky cove. Follow the sheep tracks above a series of wave cut platforms to the 82 ft high lighthouse. This was built in 1912 by David Stevenson (cousin of Robert Louis). Follow the road to the first bend then take the short, good path above the sea leading to a tiny inlet and the remains of a jetty, and winching and pulley equipment. Until the road was built in 1962, access to the lighthouse was purely by sea and all supplies had to be winched ashore.

To continue along the coast, follow the rather muddy and rough, but very useful sheep tracks which run excitingly close to the cliffs and afford wonderful views of this striking coastline *(though no place for vertigo sufferers).* There are many tilted wave cut platforms with their distinctive volcanic layers clearly visible. Numerous shags colonise their tops. Amidst glorious aquamarine coloured shallows, lie two eye catching needle like sea stacks and several massive lichen covered block stacks. One of these has a natural arch, another a narrow keyhole where an arch is still forming; its ledges abuzz with nesting kittiwakes, fulmars and shags. The increasingly tall cliffs rise up to grassy moorland bedecked in bracken, heather, houseleeks and tormentil. Far reaching vistas open out to the coast and

104

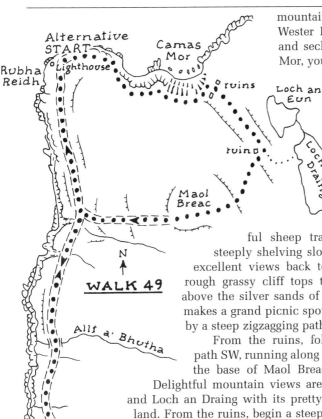

mountains of Assynt and northern Wester Ross beyond the beautiful and secluded sandy bay of Camas Mor, your next objective.

About 0.5 mile from the lighthouse, the sheep tracks descend steeply to a stream which has to be crossed below a series of small falls. Climb the straightforward cropped grass and heather to regain the cliff tops. More useful sheep tracks appear, rimming the steeply shelving slopes of a narrow cove with excellent views back to the stacks. Descend the rough grassy cliff tops to reach the ruined crofts above the silver sands of Camas Mor. The bay itself makes a grand picnic spot and can be reached easily by a steep zigzagging path closeby.

From the ruins, follow the occasionally wet path SW, running along the Loch Maree fault line at the base of Maol Breac to another ruined croft. Delightful mountain views are fronted by Loch nan Eun and Loch an Draing with its pretty fringing deciduous woodland. From the ruins, begin a steep rising grassy traverse onto the plateau of Maol Breac, aiming for the communication masts west of the true summit. The plateau comprises peat groughs and marshy hollows which necessitate a drunken course to keep your feet relatively dry. The continuing excellent prospect of the coast and mountains beyond a myriad of glistening lochans and bog pools, make a little bog hopping more than worthwhile. From the masts it is now plain sailing. Simply take the tarmac service road down to the lighthouse road and follow this back to your car, enjoying the continual vistas of Skye and the Outer Hebrides.

FACT FILE
Distance from Melvaig: 10 miles, 400m/ 1312ft of ascent, 5 hours
From Rubha Reidh: 6 miles 3.5 hours
Start/ Finish: Either Melvaig GR740871 or Rubha Reidh GR 740919
Remarks: Map & compass essential – Maol Breac plateau very confusing should mist descend.
Lighthouse Tea-room *open 12 – 5pm Sunday, Tuesday & Thursday. For details of accommodation tel. 01445 771263*

50 FLOWERDALE GLEN WALKS

The pretty Flowerdale Glen by Gairloch, was so dubbed by Sir Alexander Mackenzie, the 9th laird, given the proliferation and variety of wild flowers to be found here. Much of its beauty also stems from the wealth of fine trees from monkey puzzle, Douglas Firs and copper beeches to the large acres of native species which include Scots pine, birch, oak, willow, holly, alder and rowan. These natives have been planted as part of a policy to recreate an area of ancient Caledonian Forest. Pine martens can often be seen and to a lesser extent, stoats, weasels and otters , plus a host of birds varying from grey heron and dipper to buzzards and pipits.

The glen provides walkers with a choice of attractive routes depending on weather and/or ability and inclination. Two easy routes are way-marked by the estate, the third is much rougher and is aimed at hillwalkers. All routes include the spectacular Flowerdale Waterfalls and begin at the car park across the river from the 'Old Inn', opposite the road to Gairloch Harbour. Turn right out of the car park and follow the private road into the glen (signed for the falls).

A – The Way-marked Red Route – 2.25 miles (allow 1.5 hours) – *an ideal wet weather outing*
The road passes close to Flowerdale House. Although only built in 1738, Flowerdale has been the seat of the Mackenzies since 1494, when King James IV granted them the lands. This followed over 200 years of conflict with the Macleods after the ousting of the Vikings from this territory in 1263. Nearby, the White Barn is the oldest dated barn in Scotland, built in 1730. When the tarmac ends, a gentle and well made track continues upstream past one bridge. It reaches the first of the waterfalls above a second bridge recently constructed by the army, over a confluence of the Easan Bana and River Ghlas. This is the end of the red walk and you must retrace your steps. However, this misses a number of other falls on the Easan Bana, the stream on your left. The first of these can be partially seen from the bridge. To explore further, cross the bridge and take the main path for a short way, before forking left onto a narrow path climbing above the right bank of the river. Over the course of about 0.5 mile, there are a whole series of impressive falls plunging from Loch Airigh a' Phuill. *Note that this path is often wet and quite slippery, and is inadvisable for young children.* (Do not be tempted by another narrow path on the left bank of the river, starting at the bridge. It is exceedingly steep, slippery and highly treacherous and because of tree cover, affords poor views of the falls).

B – The Way-marked Blue Route – 3.25 miles (allow 2 – 3 hours)
This follows the red route to the falls, then backtracks to the first bridge. A forest road climbs easily to a viewpoint offering a fine prospect to Loch Gairloch and The Minch. The track heads through the old farm land and onto a second viewpoint on An Torr (Cherry Hill) which affords vistas of the hills surrounding Flowerdale

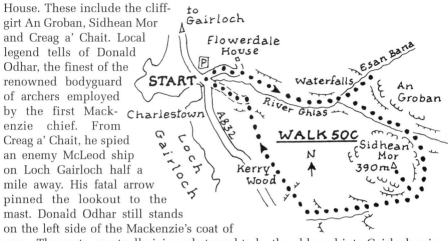

House. These include the cliff-girt An Groban, Sidhean Mor and Creag a' Chait. Local legend tells of Donald Odhar, the finest of the renowned bodyguard of archers employed by the first Mackenzie chief. From Creag a' Chait, he spied an enemy McLeod ship on Loch Gairloch half a mile away. His fatal arrow pinned the lookout to the mast. Donald Odhar still stands on the left side of the Mackenzie's coat of arms. The route eventually joins what used to be the old road into Gairloch prior to 1846, now a track which is inclined to be muddy. This returns you to the 'Old Inn', the oldest hotel in the village built around 1792.

C – Sidhean Mor 390m / 1280ft & Kerry Wood

This circular route is for the more adventurous walker who wishes to reach an even finer viewpoint than from the blue route and explores the surprisingly wild country beyond the waterfalls which is in stark contrast to the lush greenness of the lower glen.

Having viewed the upper falls on the Easan Bana as per **walk 1**, retrace your steps to the 'army bridge'. Take the path above the left bank of the right hand stream which climbs past the waterfall into the upper Flowerdale Glen. The path follows the river for about 400 yds before swinging away to the left to a stile over the deer fence. Across the stile, continue up the valley on a rather marshy path. Enclosed by an arc of seemingly impregnable craggy hills, the glen is very reminiscent of rugged Knoydart on a miniature scale. Eventually on your right, the slabby cliffs of Sidhean Mor begin to fall back. Find a suitable place to cross the river and climb the heather and grassy slopes below the base of Sidhean Mor's crags. In late spring, a mass of orchids and butterwort provide an explosion of colour, replaced in summer by sundews, heather, bog asphodel and yellow saxifrage. In the distance, the river splits into an attractive series of ribbon falls tumbling over rocky ledges.

In clear weather, an optional ascent of Sidhean Mor is possible. Keep following the broken slabby cliffs until breeches appear in their defences on the SE flanks. Steep and narrow grassy corridors grant access to the gentler upper slopes. There are ample (avoidable) opportunities for entertaining scrambles. The summit enjoys bewitching views out across the Flowerdale Estate to Loch Gairloch and the Western Isles and to the peaks of the Flowerdale Forest, Torridon and Letterewe.

Retrace your steps to the foot of the crags then head SW down straightforward moderate grassy slopes to gain the clear track running through the pretty Kerry

Wood. Turn right along the often muddy track . This leads back into the delightful woods of the Flowerdale reafforestation area. Keep straight on at a junction of tracks soon after the stile. On reaching a forestry road, cross over and keep straight on along the muddier track. Eventually you join the 'blue route' about 600 yards from the Inn. Across the open fields, one can really appreciate the beautiful trees surrounding the estate houses.

FACT FILE
Distance: 6.5 miles Height gain 500m/ 1605ft
Time: 3.5 – 4 hours

51 SIDHEAN MOR 225m/738ft & THE RIVER BRAIGH-HORRISDALE

Close to the bustle of Gairloch and the busy road to Badachro and Redpoint, lies a relatively unfrequented area of low craggy hills, small lonely lochans and rushing rivers on the fringes of the remote Flowerdale Forest. This varied walk ascends one of these hills, Sidhean Mor, overlooking beautiful Loch Shieldaig, before cutting across lochan studded moorland to reach an easy track and impressive gorge on the Abhainn Braigh-horrisdale.

Take the B8056 Redpoint road just south of Gairloch and park in a large lay-by at Shieldaig just past the hotel. Walk back along the road 100 yds and take the obvious track on the right, past farm buildings. Keep left at the first track junction then bear left again at a cairn, onto a rather wet path a short distance on. After some 10 minutes of steady climbing, the main path swings right across a very boggy patch. Instead keep straight on following traces of path beside a tiny burn. As height is gained, an increasingly fine view opens out over Loch Gairloch to the Western Isles. Continue to a tiny col from where lochans and the peaks of the Flowerdale Forest hove into view. Sidhean Mor lies directly above on the left, an exceedingly craggy little hill. Experienced scramblers can find a number of entertaining routes up. Ordinary walkers however will find only one breech in its defences above the lochan. Follow the indistinct path which swings left around the base of the final cliffs and appears to be leading to an apparent tiny col between two sizeable crags. Some 50 yds before this 'col', look to the left for the traces of a path which becomes clearer nearer to the summit. There are a few feet of easy scrambling on good clinging rock, otherwise it is straightforward walking. The summit trig point is quickly gained which affords a superb prospect to the Outer Hebrides beyond Badachro Harbour and to a fine arc of rugged peaks encompassing the Flowerdale, Torridon, Letterewe and Slatterdale Forests.

Return to the lochan and follow the right hand shore westward (traces of path) to pick up a well defined though very peaty path which now turns south to a V shaped lochan, the first of the Lochan Sgeireach (the Fairy Lochs) and swings left under a crag. A plaque is fixed to the crag in memory of the 15 people killed on 13 June 1945 when an American Liberator aircraft crashed here in poor visibility. Much of the wreckage can still be seen and should be left alone as a mark of respect. Leave the main path just beyond the crash site and keep heading south, following the shore of the most easterly of the pair of lochans. This lochan is adorned with lilies and red throated divers can often be seen feeding here. Breasting the small rise ahead, views open to Beinn Alligin and the Flowerdale Corbetts. Descend to the lochan ahead, shaped rather like a crucifix and follow its northern shore to the SE corner. A SSE course over easy moorland gains the good track at a ruined shieling beside the lively Abhainn Braigh-horrisdale. By taking the clear track to the right, Shieldaig is easily reached in 2.75 scenic miles. However, it is worth a detour for a further 0.5 mile upstream to appreciate a pretty wooded gorge and waterfalls; a green oasis in stark contrast to the bleak moorland above and below. (The really energetic can continue for a further 4 miles along the track to isolated Loch a' Bhealaich for a close inspection of craggy Baosbheinn and the rarely seen northern flanks of Beinn Alligin and Beinn Dearg).

FACT FILE
Distance: 8 miles 265m/ 870ft of ascent
Time: 4 hours
Start/Finish: Shieldaig GR 807724
Stalking season: usually no restrictions
Public Transport: Gairloch – Redpoint postbus passes start, Achnasheen – Gairloch buses pass within a mile of the start.

52 POOLEWE TO FIONN LOCH

The Letterewe Estate is one of the last great wilderness areas left in the country, with estate housing only on its fringes and no roads penetrating its rugged mountain interior. This walk, mainly on good and always clear tracks, provides a flavour of Letterewe, reaching remote lochs that few visitors ever see.

Park in the car park below the imposing old stone bridge at Poolewe or closeby near the Post Office. Follow the private tarmac road along the north bank of the boisterous River Ewe towards Inveran. The pretty woodland is home to siskins, willow warblers, goldcrests, woodpeckers, treecreepers and redstart. An easy

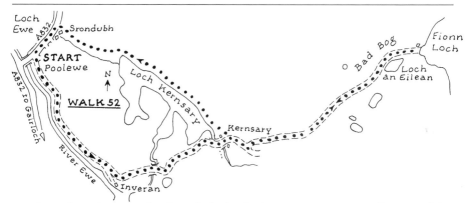

rough road continues with relatively little climbing to Kernsary. Small, craggy hills abound throughout. The estate houses at Kernsary are dwarfed by the rugged Corbett, Beinn Airigh Charr. This is a tranquil corner with the buildings fringed by birch and rowan looking out to Loch Kernsary.

At Kernsary bear left at the track junction over the stream and climb up past the cottages to a gate. Beyond the gate keep straight on up the main track, ignoring a track on your immediate left and one in 500 yards on your right. The route climbs steadily above a wide afforested strath fronting Beinn Airigh Charr and imposing Beinn Lair. In just over a mile, the track flattens out to cross bleak moorland with many glistening pools and a plethora of yellow and pink bog plants. There are increasingly fine views to Beinn Lair's striking array of cliffs; a continual wall of crags 3 miles long. Also to the thousand foot cliffs of A' Mhaighdean, the country's remotest Munro. About 400 yds past the delightful reedy Loch an Eilein, you reach the small boats moored on the dark waters of Fionn Loch. For an even finer view of this large loch, climb above the boathouse onto a small slabby hillock to the left. Don't be tempted to venture any further away from the track, the area is not called 'Bad Bog' for nothing!

The only sane way back to Kernsary is to retrace your steps. Having returned to the gate there, you have a choice of two routes back to Poolewe. The longer though easiest way is to return along your outward route. Scenically more attractive however is the alternative path which is rougher and shorter though no quicker. Bear right by the gate and follow the muddy grass alongside the dog kennels and peacock runs. Having crossed a stream, the path begins to undulate above Loch Kernsary, affording enchanting views back to the buildings and Letterewe mountains and across the loch to the Flowerdale Forest and Torridon peaks. The route is often quite wet and boggy but judicious small detours and boulder hopping avoids most of this. Turn left on reaching the main road on the eastern outskirts of Poolewe. The start point is just a few minutes away. (For those wishing to do the walk in reverse, note that the path starts a few yards west of the end of the 40mph signs in Poolewe, across a cattle grid on the left-hand side of the row of white cottages of Srondubh).

FACT FILE
Distance: 11.5 miles Height gain: 220m / 720ft
Time: 4.5 – 5.5 hours
Start / Finish: Poolewe GR 859808
Stalking season: 15 Sept – 15 Nov no access except at weekends.
Remarks: if returning by outward route, boots not essential. If returning on the alternative path, boots & gaiters advisable.

EASIER OPTIONS
The outward route to Kernsary via Inveran makes for a very easy and pleasant stroll (6.5 miles, allow *2.5 hours*). Even better, providing you don't mind bog hopping, take the rougher path to Kernsary and return via the easy private road giving a 6.25 mile circuit (*allow 3 hours*).

53 MELLON UDRIGLE CIRCULAR AND SLAGGAN BAY

This short circular walk offers extensive mountainous vistas from a delightful rocky coast with much to enjoy, even on days of relatively low cloud.

Turn off the A832 through Laide and follow the single track road north to the crofting hamlet of Mellon Udrigle. From the small, signed car park amonst the sand dunes, turn right along the road. In 150 yards bear left on to a track. About 100 yards past the first bungalow, keep stright on along a rough track when the road swings left. The occasionally boggy route, crosses heather moorland dotted with mainly new housing amidst a few ruined crofts. Ahead lies the estuary of Allt Loch a' Choire. The only noises likely to intrude on the peaceful scene are the calls of oyster catchers, snipe, curlew and sheep and the lap of the sea on the wave cut platforms and rocky promontories of the small bay. Early and late in the day, many wading birds and ducks come to feed here, including turnstones, redshanks, dunlins, whimbrels and eiders.

Having enjoyed the bay, make the short climb eastward to the cliff-top cairn on Rubha Beag. Sheep tracks assist across the cropped grass and heather. A drunken course is necessary to avoid the small, marshy hollows. The cairn looks out to the Summer Isles and the dramatic contorted coast and mountains of Coigach and northern Wester Ross. Keeping the peat groughs to your right, make for another cairn above the cliffs about 300 yards to the south east. Continue to follow above the coast, aiming for the cross atop the headland ahead. Initially it is a little rough. Rather marshy grass leads down to a charming jagged, rocky cove, home to seals, shags and graceful wheeling fulmars. From the top of the short cliffs at the head of the cove, a clear path leads onto the headland. The wonderful mountainous propect beyond Gruinard Bay is a constant companion as the path is followed easily down from the cross towards a cluster of conifers on the outskirts of Mellon Udrigle. These lie just above the pretty bay with a wide sweep of silvery sand, backed by low, rounded craggy hills and the distant serrated summits of An Teallach and Sail Mhor. The path rejoins the road to the right of the Old School House, beside the trees, less than 400 yds from the car park.

3 miles approx 260ft / 80m of ascent, 75 – 90 minutes

F or those wishing to explore the Rubha Mor Peninsula further, the above walk can be combined with the easy track to Slaggan Bay. This begins about 1.25 miles south of Mellon Udrigle, just north of the road to Achgarve. (There is off road parking just north of the track). The going is good underfoot and very gentle. The landscape of lonely lochan studded moorland gives way to the ruins of deserted Slaggan village and the peaceful, secluded sandy beach at Slaggan Bay looking out across The Minch to the Outer Hebrides. A grand spot for a picnic. *Owing to a very dangerous tide race, **do not attempt to swim in the bay**, however tempting it may appear.* Away from the track, the ground is generally rough and boggy, making a return along the track the most appealing course.

6 miles 2.5 - 3 hours

54 THE INVERIANVIE & GRUINARD RIVERS

T his exhilarating circular valley walk is suitable in all weathers. It follows the sheltered glen of the Inverianvie River; in spate a continual white water extravaganza. A short stretch of rough moorland then brings the wider and contrasting strath of the Gruinard River, well known to salmon fishermen. In addition to the fluvial interest, there is plenty to excite those of a botanical bent. (Note that the path is much rougher beyond the first waterfall, so only sure footed walkers and competent navigators should attempt the full circuit).

P ark in the large lay-by at the head of sandy Gruinard Bay, on the A832 about 1.5 miles south of Gruinard House. The Inverianvie River flows into the bay a short distance to the west. Take the obvious path above the east bank of the river. Initially it cuts a narrow swathe through the bracken beneath low, rounded craggy hills. Seas of cotton grass, sundews, butterwort, bog asphodel, orchids and marsh marigolds, are an indication of the boggy nature of the ground. Stepping stones are strategically placed over the worst of the bog. The orchids are particularly beautiful. I have never seen such a richness of variety and colour, including fragrant orchids and over a hundred lesser and greater butterfly orchids; normally only seen in ones or twos and only very occasionally.

A continual series of white water rapids culminate in the first waterfall 0.75

mile upstream. The main spectacular plunge is some 50 feet high with smaller tumbles above and below. Beyond the falls, the narrow path becomes rougher and traverses directly above the river. Having briefly descended to the water's edge, a rocky clamber then climbs above a magnificent rocky gorge, adorned with rowan, holly and birch and complete with an ebullient series of small falls. The glen unexpectedly flattens and widens out with wild peaks of the Fisherfield Forest forming a dramatic backcloth. The path across the grassy flats becomes boggier necessitating nifty boulder hopping. The river is briefly quiet. Within 400 yards, a further series of terraced falls are encountered. A little upstream, the Inverianvie now makes a sudden right angled turn. The river drops from Loch a' Mhadaidh Mor over rough gneiss platforms in two dramatic leaps.

Opposite this turn in the river, leave the path and climb briefly ENE onto a marshy shoulder. Descend the steep terraced grass beyond, to the right shore of the lochan ahead. This desolate knolly moorland can be very confusing and a compass is very useful. Climb above the lochan then follow a bearing of 54 degrees to a cairn on a small rise. Keep on the same bearing to gain a path to the left of another lochan. After a short rise, this path descends steadily to an excellent track running along the west bank of the Gruinard River. The path above is inclined to be very wet and you may prefer to make your own route down the straightforward grassy slopes to the river.

The glen is wider, with a slower and broader river, meandering between series of slabby hills which rise to the grander peaks of the Fisherfield and Strathnasheallag Forest. At two points, the river tumbles over low falls; Eas nan Sonn (GR 975890) and close to the road, Linne na Cloiche (GR 961911). There is greater avian interest here although flowers are less prolific. Orchids however still proliferate. The gentle track brings the road in 2 miles. The one mile road walk back to the start is no hardship. There is a good verge on the right side of the road with frequent views across picturesque Gruinard Bay.

FACT FILE
Distance: 6 miles Height gain: 557ft/ 170m
Time: 3 – 4 hours
Start / Finish: Gruinard Bay GR 954899 OS Sheet 19
Stalking season: Sept – Nov tel 01445 731240
Public Transport: limited buses run along A832 (Westerbus 01445 712255 & Inverness Traction 01463 239292)

EASY OPTION

The first and last sections of the main walk are suitable for anyone. The short walk along the Inverianvie River to the first waterfall, is straightforward and scenically dramatic. *(1.5 miles, allow 40 – 60 minutes, boots recommended).* The track along the Gruinard River is even easier and stretches for 6.5 miles to lonely Loch Sealga. In addition to the two aforementioned low falls, a further waterfall is passed, 3.5 miles upstream (GR 987868) (boots not essential).

55 THE ARDESSIE FALLS

D uring spate conditions, the Ardessie Falls above Little Loch Broom provide one of the finest white water spectaculars in the country. Being a short walk, this can easily be combined in one day with **walk 54**, 8 miles to the west. The going is rough and boots are essential.

P ark in the lay-by 200 yards west of the road bridge over the Allt Airdeasaidh at Ardessie hamlet. The impressive falls seen from the bridge are just a foretaste of the delights to come. A path follows up the east bank of the river, beginning about 50 yards from the bridge. This path however, is hideously wet and boggy. It is preferable to follow the rougher and pathless but drier west bank, making a rising traverse over the moorland slopes from the lay-by, to join the river above the lowest falls. The river plunges in one wide leap after another for over 500 feet, culminating in narrower falls through a deep, tree lined gorge. It is worthwhile following the river until the head of this gorge before retracing your steps.
1 mile, 820ft / 250m of ascent, 1 hour
Start/ Finish: GR 053896

56 THE TRAVERSE OF AN TEALLACH

O ne of the great sights of Wester Ross is the complex massif of An Teallach, rising above Little Loch Broom. Deeply cleaved by gullies, the tiers of sandstone atop huge scree fans, rise in heady buttresses to eroded and weathered pinnacles and castellated towers enclosing Coire Toll an Lochain, one of the finest corries in Britain. On days when clouds wreath around the numerous summits like a smouldering volcano, the mountain lives upto its name of the forge. Two Munros lie at the northern end of the traverses. They can be reached by the less experienced hillwalker. (see descent routes). The adrenaline racing full traverse of the mountain is one of the classic challenges for the more experienced. The exposed and sensational scrambling can be avoided. The traverse however, is not recommended in poor weather, especially in high winds, or under snow unless an expert mountaineer.

Park at the large lay-by at Corrie Hallie, 2.5 miles south of Dundonnell on the A832. A good track rises easily through enchanting Gleann Chaorachain, below the rough eastern walls of An Teallach. The river gorge is fringed with woodland of birch, hazel and alder. In late spring, primroses, wild roses, violets, bluebells and anemones provide a riot of colour. Several pretty waterfalls are passed near the head of the glen.

About two miles from the road, at the junction with the path to Shenevall, turn westward. Climb the gentle but rough moorland and sandstone terraces leading in a mile to the lochan under Sail Liath. Continue westward to its summit, a 1640 feet (500m) slog up grass, scree and slabs, compensated by the superb views to the majestic peaks of the remote Fisherfield Forest.

From the flat-topped summit, the excitement begins as you start out along the narrow switchback ridge, the haunt of eagles. A path drops to a col, then climbs steeply over a small pointed peak. In good conditions, scramblers with a good head for heights can continue from the next col onto the awesome Corrag Bhuidhe pinnacles. The less adventurous can take an obvious, narrow path traversing underneath all the difficulties on the south side. Beyond all the pinnacles and towers, a steep but easy scramble rejoins the ridge crest near Sgurr Fiona.

For those tackling Corrag Bhuidhe, a steep climbs brings the slightly overhanging 40 foot infamous 'bad step'. This can be turned on the left. A steep scramble up a small wall then gains the ridge crest. (Note – a rope may be useful here **and in winter one is essential**, particularly if making the traverse anti-clockwise). The giddy pinnacles rise sheer for 1000 feet above the dark waters of Loch Toll an Lochain. Although the situation is exposed, holds are good and the rounded sandstone gives excellent grip. Beyond Corrag Bhuidhe, lies the rock tower of Lord Berkeley's Seat. Its tiny airy summit leans outward over the 700 foot drop to the lochan. Lord Berkeley who was one of the first to venture onto An Teallach, sat on this point for a bet with his feet dangling out into space.

The exposed scrambling continues down to the col under Sgurr Fiona from where an easy if steep sandstone staircase leads up to the first Munro. Sgurr Fiona 3473ft/ 1059m (skoor feeana) translates as 'white or light coloured peak' from the acres of quartz screes. To reach the second Munro, continue northward along the main crest (in mist keep slightly left to avoid a false ridge). A path is picked up amongst the screes above the corrie, Mor an Teallaich. Note that this section is prone to icing. I have needed an ice axe as late as May. A steep 400 feet climb from the bealach, brings the trig point of Bidein a' Ghlas Thuill, 3484ft / 1062m, (beedyan a ghlashil) 'the top of the greenish-grey hollow'. From here, An Teallach itself is a wondrous sight, even on days when haze masks the views to Skye, the Summer Isles, Slioch, and the peaks of Letterewe, Coigach and Assynt.

The easiest descent (or ascent if just climbing the Munros) is to Dundonnell. Descend the steep and rocky ridge NNE then traverse a small rise beyond. Continue northward down an easy, broad, stony ridge to gain a path which climbs to about 750m / 2460ft. This zigzags down the steep and often rocky shoulder of Meall Garbh, reaching the road just east of the Dundonnell Hotel, some 2.25 miles from the start point.

To reduce the amount of road walking, you may prefer to descend from the col 500 yards north of Bidein a' Ghlas Thuill. Drop steeply eastward into the Glas Tholl corrie (not recommended if choked in snow) then follow down the heathery north bank of the stream. If found, an indistinct path eases progress. Beyond the Garbh Allt waterfalls, a much clearer path leads down to the road, 800 yards north of the start.

FACT FILE
Distance: 12 miles approx 4600ft / 1400m of ascent
Time: 8 – 10 hours
(2 Munros only from Dundonnell, 4550ft, 9 miles, 7 hours)

Start: Corrie Hallie GR 114850 Finish: Dundonnell GR 094877 or 112857 OS Sheet 19
*Remarks: full traverse not recommended in high winds, **for experts only in winter***
Stalking: most of the walk is covered by Eilean Darach estate tel. 01854 633203
Also check local notices as Gruinard & Dundonnell estates cover small parts of the walk.
Public Transport: Buses to Dundonnell from Inverness (via Braemore Junction) and Gairloch. Westerbus 01445 712255, Inverness Traction 01463 239292

EASIER OPTIONS

The first part of the walk through pretty Gleann Chaorachain makes for an easy and pleasant outing. Return the same way.

For those who can cope with some rougher, pathless walking, Loch Toll an Lochain is a worthy objective. Above the aprons of scree, tier upon tier of sandstone cliffs rise 1300 feet to the awesome serrated skyline of An Teallach, whilst at your feet lie glacial outwash, erratic boulders and striated rock slabs.

To reach the corrie, head up Gleann Chaoraichain for nearly 2 miles until above the waterfalls then head WNW over the moorland of heather and sandstone slabs. To vary the return, one could descend NNE into Coir a' Ghiubhsachan and follow the sandstone terracing NW, joining the path beyond the Garbh Allt waterfalls, leading to the road 800 yards north of the start.
Toll an Lochain circular 8 miles, 1542ft / 470m of ascent, 5 hours

57 ASCENT OF BEINN GHOBHLACH 2083ft/ 635m

This circular hillwalk climbs the unfrequented and isolated 'forked hill'. Being neither Munro nor Corbett, herds of red deer are far more likely to be spied than fellow hillwalkers. Lying on a peninsula overlooking both Loch Broom and Little Loch Broom, it is a wonderful viewpoint. Save it for a fine day when entrancing vistas will extend across the Summer Isles and The Minch to the Outer Hebrides and northward to the shapely peaks of Coigach and Assynt and the wild Sutherland coast. Clear weather will also avoid any potential navigational headaches. The hills are predominantly grassy with innumerable sandstone boulders and small crags. The complex ground could be confusing in mist.

For those staying in Ullapool and without their own transport, arrange to take the irregular hotel ferry across Loch Broom to the Altnaharrie Inn. A bulldozed track above Altnaharrie leads to a pass looking to Little Loch Broom. Head westward from the pass over rough, gentle moorland onto Cnoc a' Bhaid-rallaich.

For those with cars, a shorter alternative is to take the narrow single track road to Badrallach off the A832, 2 miles south of Dundonnell. There is limited parking at the road end *(ensure sufficient room is left for lorries to turn)*. Walk back along the quiet road for about 1.5 miles; an opportunity for drivers to enjoy the view across the peaceful loch to the Ardessie Falls and An Teallach and Sail Mhor. Find a grass and heather corridor free of bracken and climb NE over the moorland to around 300 metres before dog-legging back NW to gain the gentle east ridge of Cnoc a' Bhaid-rallaich; a grand high-way for viewing the loch.

From the summit, descend NNW to the broad, sandy peat col holding Loch a' Bhealaich, overshadowed by the very steep SE flanks of Beinn Ghobhlach. Swing round to ascend the easier eastern flanks of the hill. The grandstand summit is perched above the precipitous northern cliffs.

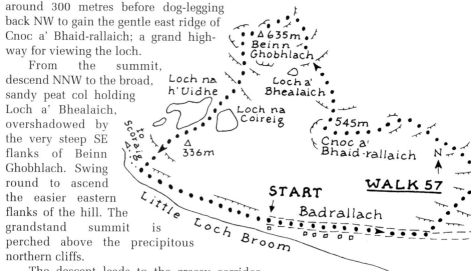

The descent leads to the grassy corridor between Loch na h-Uidhe and Loch na Coireig. You can retrace your steps to Loch a ' Bhealaich and then follow the rather marshy north bank of the issuing stream SW. Alternatively, a drier but steeper route heads down the rocky west ridge until there is a sudden break in the angle of slope. From here, descend SSW. A wide, boulder studded grassy corridor runs down the centre of the southern face, flanked by broken sandstone crags. Follow above the east shore of Loch na h-Uidhe, then ascend the slight rise ahead, immediately west of the crag girdled point 336 metres. A bearing of 222 degrees gives a straightforward if steep, grassy descent. The good coastal path running to Scoraig is joined at a small burn and provides an easy return to Badrallach. Those returning to Altnaharrie will have to continue along the road up to the pass to rejoin the outward route.

For those preferring to climb the route in reverse, follow the Scoraig track from Badrallach for about 15 minutes before making a rising traverse NW onto the shoulder immediately west of point 336m. Should you go too high and find your-self on point 336m, note that there is a break in the cliffs about 100 yards east of the cairn at a small dip in the ridge. From here, a broad grassy corridor provides an easy descent to Loch na Coireig.

FACT FILE

Distance: from Altnaharrie 13 miles 6 – 8 hours (from Badrallach 8 miles, 5 – 6 hours)
Height gain: 2690ft / 820m
Start/ Finish : Either Altnaharrie GR 115930 or Badrallach GR 057918 OS Sheet 19
Stalking season: tel. 01854 633219
Public Transport: Altnaharrie Inn ferry tel. 01854 633230 to make arrangements

EASY OPTION

The well constructed path from Badrallach runs for 4.5 miles to the remote crofting and craft township of **Scoraig**. It makes for easy walking with grand views along Little Loch Broom. You may be lucky enough to spy basking seals below the sandstone cliffs, patrolled by shags, gulls, kittiwakes and gannets. The path is occasionally a little muddy and boots are recommended. Return the same way.

58 THE FALLS OF STRONE & CUILEIG GORGE

Less than a mile from the hordes of tourists who mob the Corrieshalloch Gorge and Falls of Measach, lie the little known Falls of Strone and the foot of the Cuileig Gorge. With no fancy car parks and sign posts, virtually no-one visits here, although scenically spectacular, especially after rain. A gentle track leads to the falls. The last 100 yards are over rough, marshy grass, making boots and gaiters or wellingtons advisable. The continuation of the walk into the gorge is much rougher and only recommended to sure-footed walkers.

Park in the middle Lael Forest Garden car park on the A835 Ullapool road, about 2.5 miles north of Braemore Junction. Cross the road and take the private road over the River Broom to Auchindrean. Turn left beyond the farm buildings and take the rough track heading upstream (ignore a track leading off to the right uphill). If you would like a longer walk, this same point can be reached by driving further north along Strath More to the Blarnalearoch road then taking the track returning south along the attractive strath, on the west bank of the River Broom.

The track fizzles out less than 100 yards from the tree lined River Cuileig. Continue straight on over the flat marshy ground, liberally carpeted in orchids and bog asphodel. The falls can be seen ahead through the trees. To view the wide triple tiered falls properly, carefully descend the easy, though greasy rocky ledges and traces of path down to the river. An

119

idyllic spot. (Note that the path shown on the map leading from Braemore Square to the falls is no longer practicable as the bridge across the gorge of the wide River Broom has gone). To continue up the glen, return to the end of the track and look for the traces of path climbing through the bracken above the small gorge. At the first side stream reached, cross over and keep a little left. The path heads back towards the main river close to a bridge (now in dangerous condition) at the top of the falls, then heads upstream a little away from the gorge. Having passed through a gate, the path generally becomes more obvious, although in summer one can still occasionally lose it in the high bracken. Where the hillsides remain grassy and free of bracken, bog plants flourish, including literally thousands of bog asphodel and orchids. I have never before seen so many orchids on one walk. The route climbs steadily above the ever deepening gorge, a wider version of Corrieshalloch. It is equally tree lined and crag-girt though with a succession of small and varied falls rather than just one long one. Looking back to the head of Strath More, the scene is dominated by the rough flanks of Beinn Enaiglair.

About 0.75 mile up the main gorge a tributary gorge is reached and the site of a collapsed bridge. It would be possible to scramble up the very steep banks of the stream and cross above the gorge but high bracken makes this very awkward in summer. Better to retrace your steps and access the upper part of the gorge from the A832 Gairloch Road.

Park in the lay-by just east of the road bridge (GR 180768) about 1.25 miles west of the Strath More viewpoint car park. Make your way down the steep banking through the trees beside the lay-by, to view an impressive falls and rock stack in the middle of the river. Return to the road and go through the gate on the far side of the bridge which gives access to the more open north bank. There are traces of path above the river heading downstream, although to see the river itself requires short diversions across the rough moorland. The collapsed bridge reached earlier lies 0.75 mile downstream. Again retrace your steps.

FACT FILE

Distance: Falls & lower gorge 4.5 miles 110m/360ft of ascent, allow 2 – 2.5 hours
Upper gorge: 1.5 miles 50m / 164ft of ascent, 1 – 1.5 hours
Remarks: walk passes through sheep country, essential to keep dogs on lead

59 LAEL FOREST GARDEN

Some 2 miles north of Braemore Junction on the A835 south of Ullapool, Lael Forest offers sheltered and attractive walking, suitable in inclement weather. A collection of 150 different species of trees and shrubs from all over the world have been gathered, ranging from the small and delicate white flowered pulchras of Asia to the giant Sequois of California. Easy paths lead through the arboretum where many trees are labelled. Three easy to follow way-marked trails have been laid out in the forest surrounding the arboretum. There are three separate car parks. The central one is the best, being the start for all the walks. Boots are recommended on all trails after rain, although stout shoes are fine if it is dry.

120

THE GREEN TRAIL is the gentlest but the lower section which connects the central to the most southerly car park, becomes rather wet and muddy after rain. It is also very enclosed by trees with views limited. (0.75 mile plus arboretum, *allow an hour*).

THE RED TRAIL is steeper though on better tracks and paths. It climbs about 200 feet before levelling out and then descending steeply close to an attractive wooded gorge. It returns to the central car park through the arboretum. (0.75 mile, *allow an hour*).

THE BLUE TRAIL climbs about 400 feet to a good viewpoint over Strath More. It returns into the forest and climbs once more to cross a deep, wooded gorge at the head of a significant waterfall. It descends past several other gorges, joining the red trail near the finish and returning through the arboretum. (1.75 miles, *allow 1.25 – 2 hours*).

60 THE ASCENT OF BEINN DEARG 3547ft/ 1084m, CONA MHEALL 3214ft/980m, MEALL NAN CEAPRAICHEAN 3205ft/ 977m, EIDIDH NAN CLACH GEALA 3039ft/928m & SEANA BHRAIGH 3040ft/927m

These five remote Munros are usually climbed in the course of two or three very long day walks. More pleasurable however is to traverse all five in the course of a one and a half day leisurely backpack; in clear weather one of the finest scenic expeditions in the northern Highlands.

From Inverlael in Strath More, a private road climbs gently for 2 miles through the Lael Forest into lower Gleann na Sguaib. In spring the monotonous conifers are enlivened by a gay profusion of primroses and violets. Maps do not accurately record the forest tracks. One should take the third turn-off to the left in about a mile, crossing the river bridge and then follow the track to the right. Emerging from the trees, a good stalkers' path leads gently up the glen passing some attractive cascades on the River Lael and a beautiful little lochan nestling below the mighty glistening cliffs of Beinn Dearg's NW ridge. The going steepens for the final pull onto the broad stony col under Beinn Dearg. Follow the wall up steep grassy and rocky slopes. Where the wall turns to the west, steer SSW across the large domed plateau to the summit of Beinn Dearg, 'red hill' (byn jerrak). Views are magnificent; range upon range of mountains stretching from the Cairngorms to Ben Loyal in the far north. *It is one of the few hills from which you can see both the east and west coasts of Scotland.*

Having returned to the broad col, Cona' Mheall, (konu vyal) *'hill of the meeting'*, is reached just over 0.75mile away across easy angled grass and a mass of unstable boulders. Rocky Coire Ghranda forms a spectacular foreground with the Cairngorms a distant backcloth. Again retrace your steps to the col. A gentle grass and boulder ridge gains the third Munro, Meall nan Ceapraichean *'hill of the stubby hillocks'* (myowl nan kehpreechan) and hopefully an exquisite view down Gleann na Sguaib to sparkling Loch Broom, Ullapool and the Summer Isles. From the summit cairn, continue NE along a broad stony ridge to Ceann Garbh before descending steeply towards the col under Eididh nan Clach Geala weaving through a maze of small crags and rock bands. In mist this section would be very confusing. Even in clear weather I found myself having to backtrack several times when confronted by crags. A 500 foot pull up moderately graded grass brings the fourth Munro. There are two cairns, 100 yards apart, the one to the NW being the higher. The mountain name means *'web of the white stones'* (pronounced: aytyee nan klach gyala); frost action having created intricate quartzite geometric shapes.

More boulder strewn grassy slopes lead quite steeply down to an ideal campsite at the next col where a right of way crosses from Gleann Beag to Inverlael. The ground between here and the remote summit of Seana Bhraigh is broken hummocky moorland and more complicated than the map suggests. Steer a westerly

course aiming for Loch a' Chadha Dheirg. More straightforward grassy slopes now lead onto the SE ridge which is followed to the summit of *'old upland'* (pronounced shena vry), one of the remotest and finest mountains in Britain. I climbed it on a clear late summer evening; an unforgettable and magical experience. Thirteen hundred foot cliffs plummeted into the crater of Loch Luchd Choire. The fine corrie ended in the east with the sharp point of Creag an Duine. Innumerable sandstone peaks in Sutherland and Caithness glowed delicate pink whilst the sun danced silver on the sea near Ullapool; the Summer Isles sharply etched. The River Douchary and hundreds of tiny lochans and bog pools in Gleann a' Chadha Dheirg winked at me like sparkling jewels. Retracing my steps back to the campsite col, a vertical band of light displaying all the colours of the rainbow, glowed iridescently against a pale orange sky. Approaching camp, I startled a large herd of deer who galloped off narrowly missing my tent. A perfect end to one of the most energetic but greatest hill-walking days of my life.

From the col, a stalkers' path winds down into Glean a' Mhadaidh passing numerous lochans nestling beneath the crags of Coire an Lochain Sgeirich. The open valley permits wide ranging views to the impressive bulk of An Teallach and the Assynt and Coigach hills. The path is inclined to be boggy on occasions but is easy to follow beside the playful Allt Gleann a' Mhadaidh, somersaulting over a series of small falls. Back into the forest, an easy track leads back to Inverlael.

FACT FILE

Distance: 21.5 miles Height gain: 6500ft/ 1980m
Time: 1.5 days
Start/Finish: Inverlael, Strath More GR 183853
Remarks: good navigational skills required in hillfog
Public Transport: Inverness – Ullapool buses pass start
Stalking season: contact the keeper Inverlael Estate 01854 655274

EASIER OPTION

Lael Forest Garden – see **walk 59**

61 ULLAPOOL HILLWALK

This circular low hillwalk from Ullapool provides excellent views along Loch Broom to the surrounding mountains and the Summer Isles. It is ideal on a day when strong winds make higher tops impractical. Botanists will enjoy a moorland rich in flowering plants. The route is preferable at weekends when the small quarry workings passed on the descent are silent.

Follow Mill Street northward on the eastern edge of Ullapool to Broom Court. To the left of the court and to the right of an electricity sub-station, a signed footpath begins. The excellent well constructed path climbs steadily eastward, zigzagging above the town over moorland of bracken, gorse and wee craggy outcrops. The bracken soon gives way to heather, a variety of grasses and a colourful profusion of flowers. Squill, cotton grass, bog asphodel, milkwort, lousewort, tormentil, bugle, yellow saxifrage and a host of orchids are the most easily seen. Beinn Ghobhlach features prominently above the mouth of Loch Broom with mighty An Teallach appearing beyond lowlier Beinn nan Ban. South eastward, Loch Broom fronts Beinn Dearg, Beinn Enaiglair and the great mountain range of the Fannichs. The finest viewpoint is from the summit of Meall Mor (unnamed on most maps GR 143946). This is reached by taking the right fork at a path junction about 200ft/ 60m below the summit. This last section is not so dry underfoot and is inclined to

be boggy after rain. (The final climb can be avoided if so desired by keeping left at the junction. Both routes join later).

If you prefer to keep to paths, then retrace your steps from the summit back to the last path junction and turn right onto the path leading to Loch Achall. Alternatively, from the top descend the fairly steep pathless moorland slopes ENE towards Loch Achall. A fence is reached after several hundred yards. Turn left and follow the fence down to the path at a gate. Turn right through the gate. A gentle descent gains the quarry road 0.5 mile west of the attractive loch. Turn left. The road drops easily back into Ullapool above a picturesque gorge. The upper slopes are carpeted with birch and rowans, home to a multitude of birdlife. I set up an immature buzzard, a sparrow-hawk, a twite and wren, all at very close quarters. The lively Ullapool River remains largely hidden though parts can be seen by strategic short but steep and very careful detours off the path (not recommended with children). Along with the roadside banks of thyme, these all help to distract the eye from the ugly small quarry passed on the left. The sheds, lorries and spoil heaps passed later cannot be avoided but are quickly behind you. On reaching the main road, turn left. Broom Court is soon reached.

FACT FILE

Distance: 5.5 miles Height gain: 853ft/ 260m
Time: 2.5 – 3.5 hours
Start/ Finish: Broom Court, Ullapool, GR 132945 OS Sheet 19 & 20
Remarks: During weekdays, the quarry road above the Ullapool River is occasionally closed temporarily for quarry blasting.

The walk can easily be extended if so desired. From the western end of Loch Achall, a path climbs the gentle moorland NNW to a lonely complex of hill lochans. From their southern shore, either a path or track can be followed SW down to the A835 just north of Ullapool.

EASIER OPTION

For those preferring a gentle stroll, the shoreline north out of Ullapool provides a short, scenic outing with good views along Loch Broom. From Castle Terrace near to its junction with Quay Street, steps lead down to the Ullapool River. Cross the footbridge and a second bridge in a few yards. Beyond, at a path junction, keep left down a grassy track to a house. Pass through two gates beside the house and follow the narrow grassy path along the river. This soon meets part of Ullapool Golf Course. Follow the fringes of the course keeping near the shore. Beyond the bank of orchids and wind battered dwarf oaks beside the fourth green, one has to take to the pebbly beach. The going is straightforward for a mile from town. The pebbles then give way to rockier shore. It is possible to continue just above the sea though it is rougher underfoot. Return same way.

APPENDIX

USEFUL TELEPHONE NUMBERS

MOUNTAIN WEATHERCALL 0891 500441
CLIMBLINE 0891 333198

TOURIST INFORMATION CENTRES

Broadford (*April – Oct*) – 01471 822361
Gairloch (*All year*) – 01445 712130
Kyle of Lochalsh (*April – Oct*) – 01599 534276
Lochcarron (*Easter – Oct*) – 01520 722357
Mallaig (*April – Oct*) – 01687 462170
Portree (*All year*) – 01478 612137
Shiel Bridge (*April – Oct*) – 01599 511264
Uig (*April – Oct*) – 01470 542404
Ullapool (*April – Nov*) – 01854 612135

YOUTH HOSTELS

Armadale (Skye) 01471 844260
Broadford (Skye) 01471 822442
Carn Dearg (Gairloch) 01445 712219
Craig (by Diabaig) Achnasheen (no phone)
Glen Affric, Allt Beithe, Glen Affric, Cannich (no phone)
Glenbrittle (Skye) 01478 640278
Kyleakin (Skye) 01599 534585
Loch Lochy 01809 501239
Ratagan, Glen Shiel 01599 511243
Torridon 01445 791284
Uig (Skye) 01470 542211
Ullapool 01854 612254

SCOTTISH TOURIST BOARD
23 Ravelston Terrace, Edinburgh
0131 332 2433
To find out more about Scotland and for details of :
Golfing holidays
Leaflets on Pony Trekking & Riding Centres in Scotland
Yachting Charter Firms, anchorages & other water sports

ROYAL YACHTING ASSOCIATION
Caledonia House, South Gyle, Edinburgh
0131 317 7388

ANGLING
Central Scotland Anglers Association 53 Fernieside Crescent, Edinburgh
0131 664 4685
Scottish Anglers National Association 307 West George Street, Glasgow
0141 221 7206
Scottish Federation for Course Angling Tigh na Fleurs, Hill o' Gryfe Road, Bridge
of Weir, Renfrewshire 01505 612580
The Scottish Federation of Sea Anglers 18 Ainslie Place, Edinburgh
0131 225 7611

BUS COMPANIES OPERATING IN WESTER ROSS

Inverness Traction 01463 239292
Scottish Citylink 0990 898989
Skyeways 01599 534328
Westerbus 01445 712255

CALEDONIAN MACBRAYNE FERRIES

Armadale 01471 844248
Mallaig 01687 462403
Uig 01470 542219
Ullapool 01463 717680

Other publications from Kittiwake:

West Coast Walks – **Oban, Mallaig, Fort William & Mull**

The companion volume to this book, containing 56 splendid
walks, with routes suitable for walkers of all abilities. All carefully
researched by Pam Clark, and illustrated with hand-drawn maps
and colour photographs.
A detailed introductory section describes this beautiful area, and
puts the featured walks into context. Holiday visitors and serious
walkers alike will find routes to satisfy their needs.

£7.95

The Western Islands Handbook

Regularly reprinting since 1986, and regularly updated, this book
is now a standard work for visitors to the Western Islands of
Scotland. Fully illustrated and with detailed maps, it gives you all
the information you need to fully enjoy this magical part of
Europe.
History, landscape, flora, fauna and an insight into
present-day life are presented in Kittiwake's usual clear and
informative style. Don't visit the islands without it!

£8 95

The Outer Hebrides Handbook

Regularly reprinting since 1990, and regularly updated, this unique
guide was written by those who really know – the inhabitants of
the Outer Hebrides.
Along with a complete guide section to take you to all the outstanding sights, there are enlightening chapters on traditional cook-
ing, weaving, fishing, weather,
history, religion and daily life. Visit the islands with this book and
you will return an expert!

£7.95

Available from all good bookshops, or by mail order from
Kittiwake.